THE CHALLENGE OF CHANGE

THE CHALLENGE OF CHANGE

Curriculum Development in Irish Post-Primary Schools
1970-1984

Tony Crooks & Jim McKernan

Institute of Public Administration

First published in 1984

by the Institute of Public Administration
57-61 Lansdowne Road, Dublin 4
in association with
the Irish Association for Curriculum Development

Designed by Della Varilly

Crooks, Tony
   The challenge of change: a survey of
   curriculum development in Irish
   post-primary schools.
   1. Education, Secondary — Ireland —
Curricula
   I. Title   II. McKernan, Jim
   373.19'09417   LB1629.5.17

ISBN 0 906980 37 2

Photoset in Baskerville by Printset & Design Ltd.
Printed by Criterion Press, Dublin

CONTENTS

This book is dedicated to Kathleen Quigley as a mark of gratitude for her many services to the Irish Association for Curriculum Development.

PREFACE

Since the 1960s major changes have occurred in the education system. These have reflected the social and attitudinal changes taking place in Irish society during the period. The desire to foster equality of opportunity has opened up "free" education at second level to everyone and in the last fifteen years — the period our study is concerned with — the number of pupils at second level has more than doubled. There have been wide social and technological changes caused by economic expansion, industrialisation, entry into the European Community and, more recently, by recession and increasing youth unemployment. Schools have felt the need to adapt the traditional curriculum to meet these changes. Consequently during the period from 1970 to the present there has been a rich experience of curriculum development. Yet this development has often taken place without any clear overall policy framework.

This study describes the various kinds of curriculum development that have occurred throughout the country and, through a survey of principals, explores the value of the experience and its relevance to the future.

The project has been carried out on behalf of the Irish Association for Curriculum Development and has been supported by the Department of Education. The conclusions drawn reflect the views of the authors.

The book is a joint enterprise. Both the authors have been actively involved in curriculum development and have brought to this study their own individual skills and perspectives. Dr Crooks contributed the introductory chapter on the background and description of curriculum projects. Dr McKernan was primarily responsible for research design, computer processing and statistical analysis. The empirical studies have been jointly written. The book, as a whole, has been a collaborative effort between the two authors but would not have been possible without the support and cooperation of a host of external agents and agencies.

The questionnaire was sent to the principals of all post-primary schools in the country. We thank all those who not only replied but answered the open-ended questions at length.

At one time or another all the members of the committee of the Irish Association for Curriculum Development helped by giving their time, by commenting and by encouraging. We are particularly grateful to Kathleen Quigley, the Honorary Secretary, John McMahon and the four chair-persons of the association since the idea of the survey was first mooted — Lola Heffernan, Dermot Quish, Henry Collins and Nora Godwin.

We would also like to thank the Research Committee and the Curriculum Unit of the Department of Education for their financial assistance and comments at an early stage of the survey; Rory Hearne of An Foras Forbartha for his help with the statistical analysis; the computer centre at University College, Dublin and its advisory staff; Dr John Harris for his continuing interest in the survey and his comments on early drafts; Anton Trant and members of the staff of the City of Dublin Vocational Education Committee Curriculum Development Unit for their comments on early drafts; Jim O'Donnell of the Institute of Public Administration for his interest in the manuscript and in its publication; Julia McGeough, Ros Willoughby and Ruth Mercier for typing and retyping the book.

Tony Crooks
Jim McKernan   *Dublin July 1984*

1.

THE EXPERIENCE OF CURRICULUM DEVELOPMENT, 1970-84

Since the 1960's there have been a number of significant developments not only in terms of new subjects, materials, modes of pupil assessment but also in terms of school organisation and structures. Indeed, some would argue that the major curricular and educational issues of the last fifteen years have been about the increase of provision and the 'control' of education. How do we provide the teachers, buildings and the examinations for the increased numbers of students caused by the introduction of 'free' education and the raising of the school leaving age? Who should control community schools? Who should have control of the management boards of schools? The major issues were organisational rather than explicitly curricular. Yet during this time important and far-reaching changes have also occurred in school programmes at post-primary level.

Curriculum development takes as problematic the aims and objectives of programmes, the ways of improving content, teaching methods, modes of organising pupils for instruction and ways of evaluating the success of these initiatives. It is a multi-faceted activity and does not refer to the production of new teaching materials alone. It is 'applied' and action-oriented in the sense that it seeks to increase the effectiveness of teachers, school programmes and instruction. Curriculum development is being increasingly accepted as part of the professional responsibility of teachers and is included in most pre-service training courses.

What do we mean by the words 'curriculum development'? The shorter Oxford Dictionary defines curriculum as a 'course, especially a regular course of study as at a school or university'. A review of the literature on curriculum reveals several kinds of definition. The 1980 Government white paper on *Educational Development* offers a classic definition of curriculum in the more narrow sense.[1]

> Curriculum will be taken to mean simply the range of subjects, with their individual syllabi, that are approved for study at a particular level.

At the other end of the continuum we have the curriculum defined in a very global way such as that suggested by Johnson:[2]

> The curriculum is the sum of the experiences of learners while they are under the auspices of the school.

For some, the curriculum is what it is intended should happen in schools — it is a book such as *Rialacha agus Clár*. For others the curriculum cannot be found in a book or in any prescription — it is what actually happens in classrooms, the interaction between teachers and pupils. In this view, the hidden or informal curriculum of peer group, school ethos, etc, is included, while in the former it is usually excluded. The two views are sometimes juxtaposed: the curriculum as a book or intention versus the curriculum as classroom activity or interaction. However, they may more usefully be seen as two levels of generality of the same concept. The curriculum as intention takes its meaning only when translated into the reality of the classroom or an equivalent learning situation. The curriculum as interaction has meaning only if that interaction takes place to fulfil some intention.

·For the purpose of this enquiry we consider the curriculum as consisting of all the planned educational experiences provided by the school to assist pupils in achieving specified aims or objectives. The Open University[3] provides the following very useful definition:

> A curriculum is the offering of socially valued knowledge, attitudes and skills made available to students through a variety of arrangements during the time they are at school, college or university.

Whatever definition is used, we should remember the sentence with which Stenhouse began his book *An Introduction to Curriculum Research and Development:*[4]

> Definitions of the word curriculum do not solve curricular problems; but they do suggest perspectives from which to view them.

Curriculum development is the applied side of these definitions. Its object is the improvement of programmes and courses in educational institutions by changes in educational plans, teaching and learning. Whenever teachers seek to become clearer about their intentions, aims and objectives, or to create more effective materials or teaching strategies, or to design new modes of assessing pupils, or to evaluate programmes, they are engaged in the process we call curriculum development.

Since 1972 a number of new curriculum experiments has been piloted. There have been particular programmes introduced by the Department of Education or by regional centres such as the City of Dublin Vocational Education Committee's (CDVEC's) Curriculum Development Unit in

Trinity College, Dublin or the Curriculum Development Centre at Shannon comprehensive school. There have also been initiatives by teachers, individual schools and groups of schools under the aegis of a teachers' centre or of a vocational education committee (VEC). This movement towards the development of curriculum is healthy because it allows for differentiation of programmes to meet the needs both of urban and rural pupils and of pupils of different abilities. It is also healthy because it supports the professional role of teachers and promotes the autonomy of schools. Yet the task of curriculum development is not one for teachers alone. They should, of course, play a central role in the process but they need to be supported through inservice education, examination development and research. The point is that schools are moving into a more open curriculum environment in which they are taking more responsibility for the provision of curriculum and thus creating a greater diversity of programmes. Indeed, it is the purpose of the Irish Association for Curriculum Development (IACD), which began in 1972, to foster such development. This it has done through regular seminars and inservice courses, through its newsletter and through the publication of case studies and reports on innovation in its journal *Compass*.[5] The enquiry which is the basis of this report provides the baseline data needed to understand the experience of curriculum development in the last fifteen years.

The enquiry is concerned with the introduction of courses such as the new Leaving Certificate courses in 1969 and pre-employement courses in 1977. It is concerned with the introduction of formal pilot curriculum projects since 1972, many of which have been accepted by the Department of Education on an experimental basis as the equivalent of the traditional tests at Intermediate or Group Certificate level. It is concerned with school-based curriculum development or ways in which individual schools are adapting the curriculum to meet their own specific needs. It is concerned with the sources of support and constraint and with the organisational arrangements which foster or which hinder curriculum development. Finally, it is concerned with the future direction of change in the curriculum.

It is not our intention to present a history of Irish education during the past two decades. That task has been done by Randles[6] and Coolahan.[7] Nor is it our intention to analyse what may be called the 'mainstream' curriculum which leads to state examinations except where new subjects have been introduced. That has been carried out with regard to curriculum and policy by Mulcahy[8] and with regard to the differing provision for boys and girls by Hannon[9]. Nor is the enquiry concerned with the work of syllabus committees which have resulted in internal changes within the syllabus or, in some cases, with the complete revision of that syllabus.

Throughout the 1960's there have been many policy initiatives which altered significantly the shape of the educational system. To understand the changes within education, it is necessary to see them in the context of the wider social and attitudinal changes taking place in Irish society during the period. Coolahan[10] has summarised these as follows:

> educational change formed a part of significant changes of attitude which were occurring in Irish society generally. A notable landmark in this was the publication in 1958 of the Government White Paper on economic expansion which led to the first economic programme and changed attitudes to economic and industrial development. Economists were now emphasising education as an economic investment rather than taking the traditional view of education as a consumer service. The returns on investment in education, both individually and socially, were held to be as high as investment in capital plans. The prosperity of the modern technological society depended on the availability of an educated workforce. Increased economic growth and production in turn allowed for greater financial resources to be applied to education. An expanding economy allows for and needs an expanded education system; new emphasis was placed on slogans such as 'a nation's wealth is its people'. Further, it was felt that a society needs to draw on the full potential of its pool of talent and many commentators remarked that existing educational provision was not facilitating that.

In May 1963, Dr Hillery, then Minister for Education, announced that the government would undertake the building of a new type of school which would be called a comprehensive school.[11] He gave two reasons for this:

— the lack of educational facilities in some parts of the country
— the fact that secondary and vocational schools were being conducted as separate and distinct entities with no connecting link whatsoever between them.

These schools were to be co-educational, they were to be open to all classes, and to all levels of ability, and were to offer a wide curriculum to match the aptitudes of their pupils. In 1966, the first three comprehensive schools were opened at Shannon, Carraroe and Cootehill. In the same year, George Colley, then Minister for Education, said he did not anticipate the number of comprehensive schools would be very great. Rather his aim was that 'secondary and vocational schools, by the exchange of facilities and by other forms of collaboration, should make available the basis of a comprehensive system in each locality'.

In September 1966, Donogh O'Malley, then Minister for Education, announced that free post-primary education would be available nationwide from the following academic year.

Four years later in October 1970 a Department circular announced the concept of the community school which was seen as the development of the comprehensive school. It was to provide a comprehensive type of education to all pupils, whatever their ability, within a catchment area.

All these policy initiatives were aimed at creating equality of opportunity. *All our Children*[12] was the title of a booklet published by the Department of Education in 1969. It described the changes in Irish education and the Department's hopes for the future.

> The nation is investing heavily in its children. All these changes are necessary if we are to attain our most urgent social and educational objective: *equality of opportunity*. Every child, without exception will receive the best possible education suited to his/her individual talents. We are in a hurry to bring this about. Indeed, in the past few years we have gone a long way towards doing so. Already, we can claim that wider educational opportunities are open to more of our children than ever before in our history.

THE NEW LEAVING CERTIFICATE COURSES

The immediate results of this desire for equality of opportunity was the widening of curriculum provision. Pupils in vocational schools were allowed to sit for the Intermediate and Leaving Certificate examinations and these examinations were widened by the introduction of new subjects. Metalwork and woodwork were introduced at Intermediate Certificate level in 1966. Engineering workshop theory and practice, agricultural economics, technical drawing, building construction, mechanics, business organisation and economics were introduced either as entirely new subjects or as a revamping of existing subjects with major changes at Leaving Certificate level in 1969 and were first examined in 1971.

All secondary, vocational, comprehensive and community schools may now offer the full range of subjects at Group, Intermediate and Leaving Certificate.

ALTERNATIVE JUNIOR CYCLE PROGRAMMES

More than fifty per cent of the population of the Republic of Ireland is under twenty-five years of age and there are now almost one million students in full-time education at either first, second or third level. Two of the main factors which have contributed to the increase in the number of pupils at second level education have been the introduction of 'free' education in 1966 and the raising of the school-leaving age from fourteen to fifteen in 1972. The effect of these and other factors has more than doubled the number of pupils (to over 300,000) who attend second level schools.

In curriculum provision this has meant there is virtually 100% participation throughout junior cycle and consequently that the full range of ability is represented in schools.

In 1971 a new curriculum was introduced into primary schools.[13] The teachers' handbook notes that before the 'advent of second level education for all, primary education had to serve as the sole basis of formal instruction for a considerable proportion of people'. This led to a situation where 'education was curriculum centred rather than child centred and the teacher's function was that of a medium through whom knowledge was merely transferred to his pupils'. Now, the handbook went on to claim, the situation was different because of universal secondary education and because of the abolition of the primary school certificate, 'the teacher is no longer regarded as one who merely imparts information, but rather as one who provides suitable learning situations and who guides and stimulates the child in his pursuit of knowledge'. The handbook points out further:

> the young child is not conscious of subject barriers; he views knowledge as a key to life and his questions concerning the world around him range over the whole field of knowledge. The curriculum should reflect this attitude of the child and be seen more as an integral whole rather than as a logical structure containing differentiated parts.

During the same period there was a movement towards examination reform at the Intermediate Certificate level. This had been fostered by the establishment of a committee to study the form and function of the Intermediate Certificate examination in September 1970, first under the chairmanship of Sean O'Connor and from January 1972 under Father Paul Andrews.[14]

These three factors — the wider ability range because of the overall increase in the number of students participating in second level education, the introduction of the new primary school curriculum, and the renewed interest in examination reform — led to the establishment of three pilot curriculum projects in 1972.

In September of 1972 the CDVEC set up its Curriculum Development Unit in Trinity College.[15] The original working brief given to the unit was to provide curricula for twelve to fifteen year old pupils and the aims of its work were:

— to provide a direct link with the new primary school curriculum
— to produce curricula geared to the needs of pupils and based on their own community
— to develop new forms of assessment consonant with the aims of the new curricula.

At the same time a Curriculum Development Centre was established at St Patrick's Comprehensive School in Shannon and funded directly by the Department of Education. In September 1972 the Social and Environmental Studies Project (SESP) was initiated in the Shannon Curriculum Development Centre and the Integrated Science Curriculum Innovation Project (ISCIP) and the City of Dublin Humanities Curriculum began in the Curriculum Development Unit. In 1973, the Outdoor Education project began in the Curriculum Development Unit and the following year the Department of Education initiated two further projects — Irish Studies and Nua Chúrsa Gaeilge.

Integrated Science Curriculum Innovation Project (ISCIP)[16]

In September 1972, ISCIP was launched with eight pilot schools. In the report on the feasibility year of the Curriculum Development Unit, it is summarised as follows:

> ISCIP is a practical laboratory-based integrated science course with emphasis on pupil participation. The role of the teacher as a counsellor and guide instead of a lecturer in the classroom is a vital and basic ideal of this scheme.

Central to ISCIP is the concept of learning by doing — by experimenting and by observing. The content of the course is very close to Science Syllabus A, the difference between the two lying not in syllabus content but in the emphasis placed in ISCIP on student experiment, group work and the integration of the sciences.

At the first teacher meeting the objectives of ISCIP were worked out in terms of behavioural skills, knowledge and awareness. The units or broad areas of content (e.g. science and the scientist in the laboratory, the living and non-living world, energy systems) were then selected to fulfil these objectives.

Pupil workcards and a teachers' manual were then produced. Four units of these materials were tested in schools during the feasibility year and then revised using information collected from teachers during their testing. While this initial use of the first units was being carried out in schools, the ideas, content and actual classroom materials were being prepared for a second year level.

This process of writing, testing and revising continued until all ten units and teachers' manuals covering the full Intermediate and Group Certificate course were in operation. There were several other developments during these early years. First and most important was a series of negotiations with the Department of Education about the provision of an alternative examination within the national system for ISCIP pupils. Permission for this was granted. The ISCIP pupils took Part A of the national Intermediate Certificate paper, consisting of 30-40 short answer questions. They also took a second written paper set by the Department of Education from a bank of questions submitted by the teachers. Finally, there was an assessment by the teachers of the pupils' work in science during the year. In 1976, the first pupils took the alternative experimental examination and since then a cohort of pupils has completed the ISCIP course and taken the examination each year.

In addition to the new materials and new assessment procedures, much effort was spent in the early years compiling lists of apparatus and supplies for the laboratory. Teacher inservice work has also been a feature of ISCIP each year since it began.

Since 1977, the study materials and a science resource book for teachers have been published and are available commercially. In recent years the emphasis on development has shifted to producing alternative materials aimed at different ability levels. For example, there is a modified form of ISCIP for slow learners and a reference book to complement the published materials. Non-print materials, e.g. slides and television programmes, have also been produced.

At present, with almost 7,000 pupils taking the programme in thirty pilot schools, and with other schools using the published materials, ISCIP is the largest second level curriculum project in the country. The Department of Education has completed an evaluation of the programme. The establishment of the Curriculum and Examinations Board has expanded interest in the wider use of this programme (as it has also in the Humanities and SESP programmes).

Humanities[17]
The City of Dublin Humanties Curriculum was the other project launched in 1972. It was more ambitious in scope. It set out to provide a direct link with the Social and Environmental studies area of the primary school curriculum. Initially, this was achieved by a number of separate programmes developed within the pilot schools. These programmes linked the teaching of English, History, Geography and Civics. At the end of the second term the teachers of these programmes came together and agreed on a common programme which they would implement in the following school

year. The aims of this common programme were to build a curriculum through which the student:

— begins to create for himself a sense of identity as an individual and as a member of a community
— understands his own environment
— learns the requisite skills of the disciplines being integrated.

The first two aims are achieved by a number of studies gathered under three broad headings:

— Man in his Own Environment
— Man in a Contrasting Environment
— Contemporary Issues.

Within each of these broad headings there are further specific studies. For instance, life in the Aran Islands around 1900 forms one specific study under the heading Man in a Contrasting Environment. In the same way study of global population and resources but with particular reference to Ireland is a specific study under the heading of Contemporary Issues.

To achieve the third aim of the course the skills normally developed in the national courses of English, History, Geography and Civics were identified, listed and incorporated as appropriate into the various studies.

The schools which developed and used this programme had to make adjustments to their timetables and the deployment of teaching staff. The time to teach the programme came from the normal timetabled periods assigned to English, History, Geography and Civics (up to 30% on a pupil's timetable). These periods were then allocated to one or, in some cases, two teachers who taught the class Humanities. From the beginning, a special period of time was set aside each week for the teachers who were teaching the course to meet and plan together.

Materials for the various sections of the programme were developed in the same general way as ISCIP, though more slowly. The process was one of gathering and compiling, using, reviewing and restructuring for use in the following school year.

While the programme was being developed, regular meetings were held with the Department of Education's inspectorate. At these meetings the aims, syllabus and proposed assessment procedures were discussed in detail with a working party of inspectors who over the years have fulfilled a vital role in advising on and monitoring these developments and in organising the special examinations and monitoring the assessment procedures.

In 1976, the Department of Education accepted for experimental purposes alternative assessment procedures. These consist of written examinations, the submission of a portfolio of work, and continuous teacher assessment. The first students completed the three-year programme and the alternative assessment procedures in that year and, as with ISCIP, these special arrangements have continued each year since then.

The materials for the various sections of the programme have been published gradually since 1976 and there are now twelve different books available commercially. In addition to these books, a series of television programmes was made in conjunction with RTE and shown on Telefís Scoile under the title 'Out on Your Own'. These programmes formed part of the study entitled The World of Work. In addition to these student materials, booklets for teachers have also been written and there has been a continuing emphasis on inservice work each year.

Humanities at present exists as an alternative junior cycle programme which integrates the subject English, History, Geography and Civics. It follows directly on from the primary school curriculum, and is used in its thirty pilot schools both by students who intend to leave formal schooling at fifteen and by students who intend to enter senior cycle. The level of skills required in the course ensures that such students are able to complete senior cycle satisfactorily. Humanities, too, has been evaluated by the Department of Education.

The Social and Environmental Studies Project (SESP)[18]

This project is based in the Curriculum Development Centre at St Patrick's comprehensive school in Shannon. It is an integrated studies programme in History and Geography involving the study of the physical and social environment with the emphasis on the student's exploration of this environment. Conceptual thinking, the ability to analyse information and to form critical judgements and the development of skills are considered more important than the imparting of content. The development of the content of SESP can best be described in two phases:

Phase 1: 1972-1975 was devoted to the development of integrated studies for first-year pupils under the general title Man and His Spaceship Earth. It consists of seven themes: the first, 'In the beginning' includes a study of the universe, the solar system, the origins of the earth. 'Footprints in the sand' is the study of the development of the human race. 'A soft day, thank God' involves a study of weather and climate on the earth. The fourth theme is entitled 'Are you right there, Michael?' and is about transport. The fifth theme is about housing and is entitled 'Be it ever so humble'. The next theme, 'No place to go', concentrates on the problems involved in settlement such as pollution, endangered species and conservation. Finally, 'No man's land' is a study of man the destroyer.

Phase 2: 1975-1977 was devoted to the development of materials for

second and third year pupils under two general topics. In the second year
the general theme is 'The interdependence of people' and food, industry
and services are the three themes. In the third year, the general theme is
'Aspirations of pupils' and the pupils study the need for man to express
himself in many different forms and ways.

There is a series of booklets to cover each of the themes in the first part
of SESP. Each booklet contains the main part or core of the materials. This is
amplified through pupils and teachers deciding on their own particular
themes and through projects and group work. In the second year the pupils
use many original documents from newspapers, historical sources etc. In
the third year they carry out a large research project of their own.

Like ISCIP and Humanities, new assessment procedures were agreed
and approved for pupils completing SESP. These procedures, which were
completed by pupils for the first time in 1977, involved:

—   an objective test: this was a multi-objective test written by teachers,
    pre-tested and standardised, which took place at the end of the first
    year of the course
—   two open book experimental essay tests taken in the second and third
    years of the programme
—   the assessment of project work based on the major research study and
    assessed in five phases.

In subsequent years these assessment procedures were replaced by a new
form of examination which contains questions that are more analytical and
interpretive in nature and the pupils have access to the SESP books and
documents during the examination. There is also a question which is wide
enough to allow each pupil to use the project which he has completed as the
basis for his answer. Finally, a summary of the project is handed in together
with the written examination script by each pupil.

At present, SESP is used in twelve schools. The Department of
Education has not yet conducted a formal evaluation. It grants permission
for alternative examinations on an annual basis.

Outdoor Education Project[19]

In 1973, the CDVEC Outdoor Education Project began. Central to this
project is the idea of using the countryside as an environment for learning.
Over the years Outdoor Education has involved four main types of
activities.

First, there are school programmes. The ingredients of any such
programme include centres away from the school, transport, equipment,
and an established place on the school timetable. Typical school
programmes vary from one-day introductory courses for first-year pupils to

more demanding four-or-five-day courses for senior students. For instance, in 1979-80, 154 one-day courses, 31 two-day courses, 11 four-day courses and 7 five-day courses took place in the twenty pilot schools.

The running of successful school programmes demands skilled and enthusiastic teachers. Teacher training, therefore, has formed the second major activity of the Outdoor Education Project. There have been introductory, intermediate and advanced courses for teachers in particular adventure sports. Recently, this element of the project was more fully structured by the introduction of a part-time course in Outdoor Education which was run in conjunction with the CDVEC College of Marketing and Design and the Tiglin Adventure Centre. Course participants reached a level of personal proficiency in four adventure activities and a leadership standard in one of these activities. They also organised a school outdoor education programme during the year. The first participants have completed this course, and the course is being repeated by the CDVEC College of Marketing and Design.

The third main activity of the project has been the impetus and encouragement given to teachers who wished to use the countryside for field studies or for work projects. Field studies on sheep-farming, forestation, land use and land formation, have all been completed. A booklet entitled *Glencree — A Source Booklet* was also compiled for the use of teachers and pupils. Work projects have taken place at An Óige hostels at Tiglin and at Baltyboys. The work was carried out by classes of fifteen-sixteen year-olds. In addition to their regular outdoor education activities, the class stayed at the hostel for a number of weeks spread throughout the school year. During each week they undertook specific work tasks which in one case culminated in the construction of a garage for the hostel.

The fourth integral part of the Outdoor Education Project has been the establishment of a set of rescue procedures and the training of a team of teachers who can implement them.

Outdoor Education is now an accepted part of the curriculum in most CDVEC schools. It is carried out by trained teachers and is linked in many instances with traditional school subjects. Outdoor Education has also been evaluated by the Department of Education.

Irish Studies[20]

In April 1973 Mr Richard Burke, then Minister for Education, announced he had under active consideration:

> the possibility of introducing into the post-primary curriculum a course of Irish Studies which, while comprehending the Irish language and literature would not have a restricted linguistic

orientation and would encompass such matters as social history and traditions as well as the evaluation and appreciation of the various cultures which have gone into the making of modern Ireland.

The resulting course was ambitious and full of potential. In the proposal and draft syllabus which were produced during the following year, it was designed as:

> an interdisciplinary curriculum structure, embodying a complex of related knowledge and skills, and adaptable to the needs and potential of different regions within Ireland, to different student age levels and to different types of student ability. Its subject matter, very broadly, was to be the life and culture of the Irish people and was to be seen and studied in the context of the broader European civilisation of which it formed an integral and important part. Finally, while it was a prime aim of Irish studies to give the student access to his cultural heritage, it was also aimed at helping him to understand and cope with the vast social, economic and cultural changes that are happening around him, and thus to play a creative role in making the Ireland of tomorrow.

The draft syllabus contained themes such as 'Ireland: the physical environment,' 'the evolution of Gaelic Ireland', and 'modern Ireland'. It showed how these themes could be taught at three levels, that of the region, that of Ireland and that of Europe. It also included a number of topics from each level for each theme which integrated the subjects history, geography, civics and one other subject in the timetable. This was the compulsory core of the subject and there was also to be a series of options. Meetings of teachers and school principals were held and there were seminars and workshops to discuss different aspects of the proposed course. Six schools undertook Irish Studies for first year as a pilot experiment and the plan was that it would build up gradually to alternative assessment at Intermediate Certificate level. Unfortunately, this never happened and despite the interest created, Irish Studies failed to achieve its potential. There are many reasons for this. They include the fact that the pilot schools were scattered and not grouped regionally as in the other projects. They were also without the advantages of a full coordination and back-up service such as that provided by the CDVEC Curriculum Development Unit or the Curriculum Development Centre at Shannon. Finally, there were problems over the assessment of Irish Studies that could not be resolved. As a project, Irish Studies is now in 'cold storage' though individual schools continue with their own Irish Studies programmes and with adaptations of the original pilot scheme.

Nua Chúrsa Gaeilge

At the same time as Irish Studies was introduced, the Minister decided to introduce a third Irish junior cycle course — Nua Chúrsa Gaeilge — to cater for those pupils not adequately served by either of the two existing courses — Bun Chúrsa and Ard Chúrsa. This new course was to complement Irish Studies. Some schools piloted both courses simultaneously. Most participated in only one of the two pilot experiments.

The main aim of Nua Chúrsa was to improve the pupils' conversational ability and to improve their attitude to the Irish language. As with Irish Studies the syllabus contained a core with various additional optional modules. In Nua Chúrsa the syllabus was entirely oral and carried 60% of all the marks in the final assessment. It used what is called the 'defined language content' approach. Certain targets or tasks which the pupil should be able to perform were defined rather than texts prescribed. In addition to the core oral language component, each pupil participated in three optional modules for assessment. Drama, music, singing, dancing, environmental studies and story-telling were all included in the list of options and it was possible for these to be taught through the medium of English or Irish as appropriate to the pupil.

Eighteen schools participated in the pilot experiment which ran for three years and resulted in an alternative form of assessment at Intermediate Certificate level in Irish. In this assessment, 60% of the marks were awarded for oral Irish, 10% for each of three optional modules and the final 10% for the teacher's impression of the pupil's effort and improvement in attitude to the language. One of the optional modules was written work and a set examination was produced for this. It is interesting to note that all but one of the pilot schools took this module.

Nua Chúrsa differed from the other pilot curriculum experiments described above in that it did not follow what is called a lock step approach. In other words, after the pupils had completed the first year of the course they proceeded to the second year, but the course was not refined and repeated at first year level with a different cohort of pupils. This meant that after three years the original group of pupils in the pilot schools completed the course and the experiment came to an end. No formal evaluation of the programme was undertaken, but the reaction from the participating schools was very positive.

TRANSITION FROM SCHOOL TO ADULT WORKING LIFE PROGRAMMES

Throughout the 1970's there was growing criticism of the education system and the way schools prepare pupils for working and adult life. The necessity for schools to be aware of industrial needs and manpower planning was perhaps first identified by Dr Hillery in his 1963 speech. A balanced curriculum would be offered in the new comprehensive school and he claimed:

> Secondary education is only one stream. What we really need in this country is the other stream, the technical and scientific.

The OECD report, *Investment in Education*,[21] offered a wider view of what education was about and was a watershed in educational development. The report sought to forecast manpower planning needs and develop strategies for education to meet these needs. The idea behind the report was that by investing in educational provision the country would be investing in one of its most important products, the pupil. Moreover, by giving status to the technical, commercial and business studies courses in schools through their acceptance at public examination level and through the establishment of regional technical colleges throughout the country, the rates of participation in these courses would increase and this would help the process of industrialisation and manpower planning in Ireland.

During the 1970s as the speed of change increased, the gap between school provision and the perceived needs of industry and society also increased. Criticism of the relevance of the education system as a preparation for work and for adult life continued to grow. In 1980 the manpower consultative committee in its *Report on Youth Employment*[22] stated:

> a comprehensive examination of the educational system regarding its relevance to modern employment of a technical nature should be carried out.

Even within education itself there was growing agreement on the necessity for change. The 1980 White Paper on *Educational Development*[23] stated:

> one broad area for discussion is the education of pupils who intend to leave school at 16 or 17 to enter the world of work. It is felt that the present Leaving Certificate courses are not always of real value to such pupils and that alternatives are needed.

In 1973, Ireland had become a member of the European Community Throughout the EEC there was growing concern with the problem of unemployment among young people as well as with the need to explore and develop new approaches to the preparation of young people for adult and working life. There was also the desire to extend cooperation and the transfer of experience between the member states in the field of education. In December 1976, the Council of the European Communities and the Ministers of Education meeting within the Council adopted a resolution concerning measures to be taken to improve the preparation of young people for working life and to facilitate the transition from school to work. Two of the outcomes of this resolution were the introduction of pre-employment courses in schools in 1977 and the establishment of a European network of pilot projects in the transition from school to adult working life in 1978.

Pre-Employment Courses[24]

In April 1977, the Department of Education circulated all vocational, community and comprehensive schools with details of pre-employment courses and invited applications from schools interested in running one. Guidelines setting out the details of the course that had been designed were circulated later and interested schools were invited to send a participant to an inservice seminar during the summer of 1977.

The guidelines stated:

> pre-employment courses are intended for students who would ordinarily leave school on attaining school-leaving age. The general aim of these courses is that of bridging the gap between the values and experiences normally part of traditional education and those current in the adult world of work.

There are three broad sections in the courses:
— technical modules
— general studies including personal and social development
— work experience.

Originally, there were nine technical modules listed and each school was encouraged to choose two from the list. Subsequently, the number of modules offered was increased to fifteen. Schools were also encouraged to develop their own modules where local conditions permitted or made such developments necessary. The general studies section comprised courses on communications, social mathematics and industrial/social studies. It aimed to develop the pupil's standards of communication and mathematics to the level required in work and in everyday life. Personal and social development was considered integral to the course. In this section the careers teacher set out to develop in the young person the ability to make career decisions, to understand himself, his capabilities and interests and to match these with the realities of available opportunities. In the work experience element pupils were placed in employment for the equivalent of one day per week throughout the school year.

At the end of the course each pupil received a course record which contained a certificate outlining the programme followed and the pupil's progress in it, references or notes from the employers and other items as appropriate. In 1977 some eighty schools organised courses and the most popular technical modules were basic construction, industry skills and light engineering. In the following year the number of participating schools rose to about 120 and has remained at about that number. In May 1984 the Department of Education issued a circular to all second level schools inviting them to participate in a new programme to be known as the Vocational Preparation programme. This programme will expand existing provision for pre-employment courses and extend them to selected secondary schools.

Shannon Project of Interventions for Relevant Adolescent Learning (SPIRAL)[25]

A second outcome of the 1976 Council resolution was the establishment of a network of twenty-nine projects throughout the European Communities. The Commission established a Central Animation and Evaluation Team (CAET) to assist in the development and evaluation of these projects, three of which were located in Ireland with the approval of the Department of Education.

The overall aim of SPIRAL was to enable the school, the home and the community in general to cooperate in the creation of an expanded learning environment that would be more conducive to the growth of adolescents from the dependence of childhood to adult responsibility. During its feasibility year in 1978, SPIRAL identified twenty-nine interventions which might help in the transition from school to working life. However, the three which the project team subsequently concentrated on were community-based learning, mini-companies and local liaison groups.

In a community-based learning programme the pupil spent between fifteen and twenty hours each week out and about in his local community following an individualised learning programme tailored to meet his own particular needs and abilities. Although the programme was individualised, all pupils were expected to acquire certain skills which were considered important for every person. These skills were categorised as core skills which enabled the pupil to grow as a person, as a member of a family, as a worker and as a citizen. In addition the pupil acquired skills considered by the local community to be necessary for adults to function effectively in that community, and basic skills that included reading, communications, mathematics and career development skills.

In a programme each pupil also undertook a number of career explorations, and a series of what were called learning ventures. The purpose of a career exploration was to help the pupil to practise critical thinking in examining his own experience and to learn about a specific job related to his own interests and abilities. Learning ventures were longer. They lasted three to four weeks. There was a series of activities undertaken for an adult in the community who acted as the pupil's tutor.

The second main intervention in SPIRAL was the establishment of 'mini-companies'. A mini-company was a legal company established by a group of pupils. The pupils went through the correct procedures for the establishment of a company, sold shares for small amounts of money. They decided on a product, manufactured, tested and marketed it, sold it and, eventually, some months later, wound up the affairs of the company. Through participating in a mini-company the pupil learnt a whole range of important skills.

The third main initiative of the project was the development of local liaison groups of parents, teachers, employers, trade unionists and representatives of interested people in the community. Such groups operated as a link between the school and the community and helped mobilise resources in the community for both the community-based learning and the mini-company.

The pilot phase of SPIRAL lasted from 1978 until 1982. During the project there was a full external evaluation and this evaluation in addition to the project reports and other documents forms part of what is called the 'national dossier' on initiatives taken by the Irish projects in the European network on transition from school to adult working life.

Education for Development[26]
The second project within the network was located in the North Mayo area and was called Education for Development. The project differed from most other curriculum development projects in Ireland in that its primary impetus came not from local schools or an education authority or from the Department of Education but from the work of the Galway/Mayo Regional Development Organisation and the Irish Foundation for Human Development. Prior to 1978 when the project began, the foundation had already worked with the regional development organisation on surveys and had found that the career aspirations of pupils in the area were very different from the type of jobs available. There was also interest in the impact of industrialisation in the North Mayo area. Loughlin Kealy, who was chairman of the management committee of the project, has described its aims as follows:

> the project 'Education for Development' has been centrally concerned with the nature of the learning experience at second level. It has taken the view that there is a deeper purpose in schooling at secondary level than the assimilation of information through the various subject disciplines, and that this deeper purpose concerns the development of

the students' ability to learn. So it has not been concerned with introducing special programmes aimed at specific sub-groups. It has been concerned with the core curriculum and how it can be developed so as to cultivate the creativity of the students. It has taken the view that the transition from school to adult and working life is part of the process of maturation for the student, and that the schooling system has an important role to play in this process. The key to its role lies in what it promotes as learning.

The project team produced three kinds of intervention to develop the pupils' abilities to learn. The aim of these interventions or series of classroom lessons was 'to invoke and integrate the intellectual, emotional, physical and spiritual capacities of the students in the learning experience'.

The first intervention was called 'orientation activities'. It involved meditational activities which helped the pupils achieve a frame of mind conducive to creative work. These were then applied by the project team and teachers in a variety of classroom situations. For example, exercises were designed to help young people participate more fully in learning activities which required a high degree of sensory involvement.

The second intervention was called 'imaging'. Loughlin Kealy describes this intervention as follows:

> The process of imaging offers access to a variety of ways of knowing, which complement and also stimulate the verbal and linear process which dominates our current teaching repertoire. Recent research into how the brain functions provides some insight into how imaging becomes a significant factor in developing the ability to think and act creatively. In calling into play the full range of brain centres, visual, auditory and so on, imaging promotes the development of a rich pattern of neural connections within the brain. This fact is associated with the growth of intelligence. In terms of hemispheric specialisation — the propensity of the two sides of the brain to act in different and complementary ways — imaging provides an active role for the right hemisphere thus developing intuitive thinking abilities and stimulating creative action. (The left hemisphere is associated with linear and analytical thinking processes.)

Lessons which incorporated this process were developed and introduced into such subjects as languages, art, mathematics and science.

The third type of intervention was called 'movement'. This took two different though related forms. The first was the use of body movement as an expressive form and the second was the introduction of special exercises designed to stimulate learning through the development of body awareness.

A number of psycho-physical exercises within the Department of Education's syllabus for physical education was devised in this intervention.

There were ten schools involved in the Education for Development project. The project team was centred in Ballina. In addition to the interventions described above the team organised seminars and workshops for teachers in areas such as pastoral care, team teaching and the impact of micro-technology on employment. At the end of the project a dissemination seminar was held and the reports from the project together with its external evaluation form part of the national dossier.

The Early School Leavers Project[27]

The third Irish project in the European network began in 1979 and was located in the CDVEC's Curriculum Development Unit. The project aimed to identify potential early school leavers and to design, implement and evaluate a curriculum suitable to their needs. Early school leavers were defined as those pupils who derive little or no benefit from their schooling, who leave school at the earliest opportunity, who are unfitted for the world of work, and, consequently, who either drift from one job to another, or remain more or less permanently unemployed. Throughout the project the team accumulated evidence and attempted to refine this definition. As a result of the research and of their own activities in the pilot schools the team suggested that within the school context the following five indicators were useful in anticipating early leaving:

—   poor attendance
—   low motivation
—   disimproved performance
—   older age
—   lack of family support.

The team stressed that:

> these are only indicators and that the non-school factors are probably of even greater importance. The problem of early school leaving is so complex that the appearance of all five indicators will not necessarily mean that the student will leave early; nor will the absence of all five indicators mean the student will not leave. However, principals, staff and counsellors who are aware of these indicators and of their interaction are more likely to be be in a position to work positively with potential early leavers in their school.

Schools were encouraged to discriminate positively in favour of these types of pupils through the allocation of additional resources. During the project three types of school programme emerged. Some schools drew up an entirely new curriculum without reference to any examination or national certificate. Others maintained a small core of subjects which are taken to Group Certificate level while the remainder of the programme was not examination based. The rest followed a more or less normal Group Certifiate programme but added significant interventions during the course of the school year. All these programmes led to an alternative type of certification developed by the project which was called the junior cycle school certificate and was awarded by the CDVEC. All the programmes contained aspects from a social and health programme, a work exploration programme, a design approach to practical subjects and an outdoor education programme. This certificate, which was awarded to the pupils, was based on a profiling system. Each teacher maintained an ongoing 'profile' of each pupil's progress in the development of basic skills as well as personal and social skills. Profiling was considered an integral part of each of the school programmes and helped the teachers to develop non-cognitive skills and to encourage pupil development in those areas by appropriate programme activities.

During the course of the project twenty-one different work exploration exercises were carried out. Work exploration was the structured introduction of young people to various aspects of the world of work and adult relationships. It involved the removal of pupils from the school atmosphere and their placement in a simulated work environment; this controlled setting was used as a base for educational and vocational discovery, discussion and reflection.

The primary function of work exploration programmes was to develop those personal and social skills which were considered important for the world of work and adulthood. The out-of-school atmosphere gave rise to a new enriching relationship between teacher and pupils and between the pupils themselves.

Each work exploration programme had three main elements:

— a preparatory component done in the classroom.
— a production component of full-time work simulation over a five-day period.
— a follow-up component consisting of the distribution of products which had been made and reflection on the experience gained.

In each experience the actual production of items was an important element as it gave a sense of motivation and achievement to the pupils. However, the actual process of exposure to a new kind of learning experience and to the personal and social aspects of work was considered equally important.

The Early School Leavers Project also developed a short ten-week programme for young people who had recently left school and were in employment. These young people were released by their employer and returned to school to participate in a programme which lasted for one half-day per week. The broad aim of this programme was to provide young people with the skills and knowledge necessary for them to succeed in life — in other words to help them acquire a greater understanding of the world of work as well as to help them in their personal development. The programme consisted of ten topics each of which developed either the work-related skills or the social and life skills of the participants.

The project ended in 1982. There was a dissemination seminar the proceedings of which were published under the title *Educational Achievement and Youth Employment*. The various project reports and the external evaluation are part of the national dossier.

Other Recent Transition Type Programmes

In July 1983, Gemma Hussey, TD, the Minister for Education, announced that Ireland would be participating in the European community's second transition programme of pilot projects, and that three of these projects would be located in Ireland: in Dublin, Galway and Shannon.[28]

The Dublin Inner City Education Project is located in the CDVEC Curriculum Development Unit, Trinity College. The aim of the project is the social and vocational preparation of young people with poor prospects of employment so as to enable them to acquire a degree of independence in a changing society. The project is primarily oriented towards three target groups:

— young people completing their schooling with poor employment prospects
— young people who have just left school and are unemployed
— girls and young women with poor employment prospects.

The project is continuing the work initiated by the Early School-Leavers Project in developing alternative junior cycle programmes which culminate in the award of the junior cycle school certificate folder. With the help of local community groups and statutory bodies, the project team have also developed a course for unemployed young people which aims at developing the young person's self-confidence and employment skills. The project team have also developed a programme for young women in the inner city.

The project for the integrated provision of education (PIPE) is located in the town of Galway Vocational Education Committee. The main aim of the project is to change the attitudes of pupils, teachers, parents and the community through the utilisation of the out of school environment. The project has contacted some thirty schools and following consultations and suggestions from principals and staff has developed five curricular interventions under the following headings: caring for your community, cooperative community enterprise, technology, the working world and taster courses.

The third Irish project is located in the Curriculum Development Centre in Shannon. Its aim is the development of new two-year post-compulsory programmes in second level schools, particularly for those pupils unlikely to succeed well in the existing Leaving Certificate. The programmes aim both at personal development and at an acquaintance with, and some skill in, a number of industrial, agricultural and commercial fields. The project is also developing a new flexible form of assessment and certification for these programmes. The content of the programme draws heavily on the experience of the SPIRAL project in using community-based learning, mini-companies and voluntary service in the community for the development of personal and inter-personal skills.

In addition to the projects described above, there are others initiated by an individual school or by a group of schools whose aim is primarily to aid in the transition from school to adult working life.

In County Tipperary (North Riding) Vocational Education Committee's schools there is an alternative mathematics course at senior cycle level. This course arose from the policy document *Post-Primary Education 1985-2000 and its Relevance to the Economy*.[29] The project began in 1979 and aims at producing an alternative course which will be recognised as an appropriate terminal qualification for pupils of ordinary ability who complete the senior cycle. The two-year course is built on a core of essential mathematical skills which forms the first part of the course and broadens out to a wider and more mathematically significant syllabus in the second part. Particular attention is devoted throughout the programme to supplying the appropriate motivation and context for mathematics and its applications. The course is based on a concept of mastery learning. Confidence in the learner is developed by the completion of many examples of mathematical problems related to work situations and other relevant applications. The first pupils completed the course in 1981 and were awarded a certificate by County Tipperary (North Riding) VEC. The course is now recognised by AnCO for purposes of apprenticeship.

Dublin City has also developed, through its Curriculum Development Unit, career foundation courses.[30] These are two-year senior cycle courses. The aims are to prepare pupils for direct entry to the world of work and to lay a foundation on which the pupils can proceed to further studies at an appropriate time in their careers. The courses are developed on a modular basis with each course consisting of a number of core modules in the area of specialisation for the particular foundation course together with a number of other related and general education modules. Work experience is also part of these courses. The courses which specialise in engineering, business studies and design and production (workshop and small industry) have been developed and implemented by individual schools. The assessment procedures for these courses consist of terminal examinations and coursework assessment. Each pupil is awarded a folder which describes the course and the pupil's performance and aptitude in each subject area. The COVEC also awards a Career Foundation Certificate to pupils who satisfactorily complete the course.

PERSONAL DEVELOPMENT TYPE PROGRAMMES

Since the early 1970's there has been a growing concern about the overall balance of the curriculum provided in second level schools. In 1977, the Irish Association for Curriculum Development issued a policy statement *Establishing Priorities in the Curriculum.*[31] The association identified six principles which 'should form the basis for a fundamental, complete and ongoing review of the curriculum'. Two of these principles are that the curriculum should cater for the needs of all students and that the curriculum should be responsive to the needs of society. Part of this statement reads as follows:

> Since children have different abilities, aptitudes and interests, no one programme can be suitable for all. The Association, therefore, promotes the concept of a comprehensive curriculum: that is, a new curriculum which has elements that are shared by all, but which allows for the development of all aspects of a child's personality and caters for different abilities. Such a curriculum would allow each child to develop to his/her full potential in all dimensions — the moral, social, spiritual, aesthetic and cultural as well as the intellectual. It would seek to blend the academic with the technical, the mental with the physical, the theoretical with the practical. It would recognise that all children do not develop at the same rate and in the same way. Such a curriculum would comprise both common elements and options. It would also allow for a variety of methods of grouping students in streamed, banded or mixed-ability groups and for flexibility in learning situations including group, project or individual work.
>
> The Irish Association for Curriculum Development is concerned with the fact that the curriculum at second level has not altered to any significant extent to meet the needs of a complex and changing society. This curriculum is a subject-centred one and, as such, tends to place too great an emphasis on mastery of subject facts. While the

Association accepts the need for and the place of subjects within a second level curriculum programme, it believes that subjects should be used as resources for, rather than determinants of, this curriculum. It believes that a subject-centred curriculum pursues a limited range of objectives. Indeed, it is debatable whether such objectives are suitable for a society experiencing rapid social, economic and technological developments. Social changes require that our pupils can cope with the pluralism of values and beliefs, particularly in such areas as the family and home, interpersonal relationships and moral decision making. Technological changes require positive attitudes towards industry, the development of a wide variety of skills: scientific and manual and such competencies as initiative, personal responsibility and an enquiring mind.

In *Curriculum and Policy in Irish Post-Primary Education* Mulcahy considers that the provision of a general education as a preparation for life is the aim of post-primary education in Ireland. He goes on to identify the four major demands of living: the vocational, the recreational, the philosophical and the practical. 'To aim at preparing pupils for life is to aim at preparing them to meet successfully these various demands'. He goes on to consider what some of these demands are likely to be, and how they might be met in terms of providing a more balanced curriculum and set of assessment procedures.

The need for greater overall balance in the curriculum is also accepted in the white paper on *Educational Development* which states:

There is a demand for expansion of the second level curriculum arising from the fact that, with the growing complexity of modern living, people now entering adulthood need a whole new range of functional skills and knowledge. Accordingly, the schools are pressed to provide social and political education, health education, consumer education, education for leisure, media education, personal development education — the list keeps growing. If some educationalists believe that such matters are not really the concern of the school, a more commonly held view is that young people today need an enlarged educational experience and that the school must offer its specialist support to the formative efforts of the home and of the community at large.

Many of the programmes which have been described above attempt to meet this need for balance in the curriculum by placing an increased emphasis on the social and personal development of the pupil. We now consider a number of other programmes which exist outside the formal examination system and in which the primary purpose is the personal and social development of each pupil.

The Transition Year[32]

The transition year project is a one-year interdisciplinary programme for pupils who have completed the junior cycle. It is seen as a transition between junior and senior cycle, or, in some cases, as an extra year to ease the transition between school and the world outside school. The idea of such a year within the school curriculum was put forward by Mr Burke in 1974 to 'stop the academic treadmill and release the students from competitive educational pressures for one year.' The purpose of the project is described in *Rules and Programme for Secondary Schools:*

> The project is directed towards the intellectual, social and emotional maturation of the pupil. It is conceived as an introduction to adult education and to *education permanente*. . . the content of transition year curricula will include elements of the following: social education; moral education; education for living (including home crafts and education for parenthood, employment and leisure); philosophy and applied logic; music and the arts; Irish studies; *civilisation;* courses for students of continental European languages; visual education; media education and communication skills etc.

Each school worked out its own programme in consultation with an inspector from the Department of Education and many exciting initiatives were taken. In the first year of the project three schools participated and by 1976/77 there were sixteen schools involved. During the year Egan and O'Reilly visited all these schools and gathered materials by means of questionnaires for the coordinator of the programme, for each of the teachers, and for the sample of the pupils. Their report gives a very full documentation of the programme in each of these schools. In 1980, an evaluation of the transition year was conducted by the Educational Research Centre in Drumcondra. The report recommended that 'the present pilot stage of transition year be terminated without delay so that work can commence on the dissemination of the programme in whole or in part to other interested schools'. Since then no action has been taken by the Department of Education. New schools are not allowed to begin the transition year and gradually the number of schools which continue to offer it has dropped. In 1983, the small financial help offered to those schools which provided transition years was withdrawn.

Pastoral Care and Social and Health Education Programmes

There are several programmes which introduce the element of pastoral care and social and health education into the curriculum. The Psychological Service of the Department of Education introduced a personal and career education (PACE) programme[33] on a pilot basis in 1980. The handbook stated the aim of the programme was to develop 'needed knowledge, skills and understanding in the areas of educational, vocational, personal and social development of all students.' The programme was undertaken because of the growing awareness of the desirability of making provision for programmes of personal and social development in schools; it provided a curricular approach to guidance provision in schools. It consisted of a series of sixteen general objectives which provided the framework for the programme and many intermediate objectives derived from the more general objectives and applicable for different year levels. The general objectives covered three broad areas:

— career planning skills and knowledge
— self-knowledge
— knowledge of work and leisure worlds.

The handbook also contains checklists to help the planning of a particular school programme, notes on organisation methods, an annotated list of resources and notes and materials for the evaluation of the programme. The project began in 1980 with eight schools and was extended in the following year to other schools. It still is considered a pilot project by the Department of Education.

There is another pastoral care project organised by the Vocational Education Committee of Tipperary (North Riding).[34] This project is part of the VEC's overall curriculum policy which was agreed in 1979. It sets out to:

— ensure that aspects of education for living which may not be covered in the general curriculum are adequately treated; and to coordinate the approach of teachers in these areas
— provide a pastoral care framework for the school which will ensure that each pupil will have, and be aware that he has, access to help on a one-to-one basis if he needs it, and that the school authorities can recognise potential problems and deal with them
— help pupils participate as fully as possible in the learning experiences of the school
— contribute to the personal development of each pupil
— help pupils to relate to others.

The VEC established a working party with representation from each of its schools and a number of topics were selected for inclusion in the course. These topics included decision making, personal relationships, leisure, health education, personal hygiene, addiction, nutrition, safety, study skills, manners and etiquette, consumer education, money and school familiarisation. Materials for years 1-3 have now been developed and the production of these has been supported by the Mid-Western Health Board and the Health Education Bureau.

In Dublin, the Curriculum Development Unit organises a Social and Health Education Programme[35] which aims to help students in:

— the development of an understanding of themselves and their growth
— the clarification of values and attitudes
— the development of an ability to make decisions which are based on consideration of the implications of their actions for themselves and for others.

Materials for junior cycle pupils have been developed and tested on the following topics:

— heredity and environment
— healthy and safe living
— work and leisure.

A final unit on growth and development is being developed.

The Health Education Bureau and several of the health boards have also provided programmes for use in schools. As the content of health education is spread throughout the curriculum through different subjects its impact depends on the choices made by pupils and on the emphasis given to it by various teachers. In 1978/79 the Bureau were involved in a pilot project with twenty post-primary schools throughout the country.[36] Among the recommendations of this pilot study was one that considered adequate materials should be provided for schools. The following subject areas were identified in the study:

— personal health, body management and human biology
— food selection
— growth and development
— relationships
— education for parenthood
— community health
— the environment in which we live
— leisure education
— safety and first aid.

As a result of this study a materials project was initiated in the Curriculum Development Centre in Shannon and five schools participated during the school year 1981/82.

The Western Health Board has its own health education programme for primary and post-primary schools. The post-primary programme consists of seven areas, and is accompanied by a handbook for teachers. The health board carries out and funds the training of teachers interested in implementing the programme in their school. Throughout the programme the approach taken is 'to encourage teenagers in small groups to come to terms with themselves, their parents and the community.' A similar type of programme entitled 'a life skills programme for schools' has been developed by the North Western Health Board.[37]

In Cork, a social and health programme has been developed since 1974 by Ógra Chorcai.[38] In the teachers' manual for the course it states:

> The programme arose initially from a concern about the dominance of alcohol in social life, about aggression and delinquency, and about drug taking. These problems encountered by young people were considered to be symptoms of underlying difficulties in personal adjustment and in social relationships, and unsatisfying patterns of recreation and leisure.

The content of this course includes studies of leisure, social values, group interaction, relationships, religious relationships, health and personality and family functions. The teaching method employed in the programme is that of experiential learning rather than lecture. Great emphasis is placed on the inservice training of teachers. Since 1981 the Southern Health Board has adopted this programme as their official health education programme at second level and it is used in most schools and also in youth clubs in the Cork area.

DEVELOPMENTS IN MODERN LANGUAGES[39]
The Council of Europe has, over the period, addressed itself to the development of an approach to language teaching which is in harmony with an emphasis on the social, emotional and cognitive development of the learner and which takes account of the necessity to equip pupils with aptitude and skills for language learning so that they can 'learn how to learn' a language in later life if necessary. The work of the Council has been taken up and applied to language learning at adult and school level in many member countries. It has resulted in a new movement which may be considered under the umbrella term 'a communicative approach to language teaching'. In Ireland, Nua Chúrsa Gaeilge, which has been described above, because of its close connection with Irish studies, used this approach. It has also been used by the Institiúid Teangeolaíochta Éireann to promote language teaching/learning. In 1978, a working party of teachers was established to investigate the possibility of implementing a communicative approach to language teaching. This approach was defined as one which:

> facilitates the use of language for communication in addition to the

study in practice of its formal aspects. Communication means using language for a purpose through activities which may involve listening, speaking, reading or writing or combinations of these skills in the performance of communicative tasks.

Later, a skeleton syllabus was drafted and the project became associated with the wider Council of Europe modern languages project. The skeleton syllabus could be fleshed out with the possible linguistic exponents for any foreign language, defining what a learner should be able to do with the language he is learning, the meanings he should be able to understand and express so as to participate effectively in situations requiring communication. Lists of grammar and vocabulary are included as essential features but these are then seen as tools the pupil learns to use rather than as an end in themselves. In other words, the emphasis is on the learner and the process of learning rather than the language.

In 1979, over two hundred teachers attended a seminar at which this 'skeleton syllabus' was presented. As a result of the seminar, and on the recommendation of the Council of Europe's modern languages project, work then began on the writing of communicative teaching materials for classroom use. Teaching materials were developed for French and German and more slowly for Spanish and Italian. The teachers involved in the project met on a regular basis and also attended inservice workshops. In 1983, the first materials and audio tapes were published and are used throughout the country.

More recently three alternative Irish programmes have been initiated. The same 'skeleton syllabus' has been used as a guideline by a group of Irish teachers working on the pilot project 'Mise agus Tusa'. In addition to the skeleton syllabus, this group have designed a questionnaire for students who use the course to give their reaction to its contents. This project is being developed by Bord na Gaeilge.

There is also a three-year programme for less academic students being piloted in eighteen schools and coordinated by the Curriculum Development Centre in Shannon. Emphasis in this programme is on oral language. It aims to produce pupils who have sufficient Irish for satisfactory communication including basic language skills and who actively enjoy the Irish language.

There is another Irish programme for urban teenagers designed to complement the Group Certificate syllabus. This programme has two elements: a series of activities and materials in language teaching produced in the form of stories about a group of urban teenagers and an introduction to aspects of Irish culture including music, folklore, legends and cultural activities. It is coordinated by the CDVEC Curriculum Development Unit.

OTHER RECENT DEVELOPMENTS
In addition to all the projects described above there have been other programmes which aim to diversify or expand the existing curriculum. There have been several media studies programmes. Some of these have been limited to one school. In other cases small groups of schools have worked together on the initiative of a teachers' centre or a VEC. The CDVEC Curriculum Development Unit, in conjunction with the Irish Film Institute, has produced materials for classroom use on imagery, newspapers and television.[40] In another case, the framework for a syllabus has been drawn up. The Curriculum Development Unit has also produced materials in the form of a series of case studies on industrial relations.[41]

In 1980 a three-year project in development education was initiated. The project was monitored by a joint committee of the Irish Commission for Justice and Peace and the Irish Council of Churches and financed by the Bilateral Aid Section of the Department of Foreign Affairs. Development education was defined by O'Flynn, the director of the project, as 'education whose main, but not exclusive focus, is life in developing regions of the world. . . it is not solely concerned with the production and analysis of facts, it is also concerned with eliciting attitudes.[42] Twelve schools were involved in the piloting of a draft source/workbook which contained the following sections:

— rich world/poor world — in which reasons for the division of the world were explained from an historical perspective and the relationship between exploitation, environmental factors and poverty considered
— a case study of Lesotho — a country which is in receipt of Irish bilateral aid
— food
— pollution
— images of people from other countries.

In 1983, the Department of Education initiated two new projects in English and History. The English project has twenty pilot schools which are grouped in regions. Its purpose is to develop alternative programmes for second and third year English, which are suitable to the needs of less academic students. Its main emphasis is on the development of new approaches to the teaching of basic language skills, creative work, media literacy and drama. The History Action Research Project also has twenty pilot schools. It is a three-year junior cycle History project which aims to involve teachers in its planning and development and to involve pupils in school-based historical research. School-based materials are being developed for two alternative courses within the project. One is a survey course from earliest times to the present with in-depth studies which will be chosen by the teacher. The other is a course on twentieth century Irish and world history plus line of development studies chosen by the teacher.

Irish schools participate in two networks which are sponsored by the European Community. Three schools participate in an environmental education network whose purpose is to create awareness of the concept of environmental education in schools, to promote cooperation between schools at a European level, to put this concept of environmental education into practice and to make available the results of this process of cooperation and mutual learning to other schools and to the public at large.[43] Two other schools participate in a similar network concerning consumer education.

There are also schools which have bought curriculum materials published outside Ireland. Materials from the early Nuffield Foundation and Schools Council projects have been used. Perhaps the most important has been the Cambridge Classics Project which has influenced the development of the new classicial civilisation course as well as the methodology of teaching Latin.

There has been a systematic adaptation of curriculum materials to an Irish setting. For two years between 1970 and 1972 an independent learning system in mathematics called IMU was used in twenty schools in Ireland. The IMU was developed in Sweden to allow pupils to work at their own pace, at an appropriate level of difficulty while remaining in a mixed ability group. The project was conducted under the auspices of a grant from Shell. The project was carefully monitored and evaluated and in many aspects was the precursor of much curriculum development in Ireland. However, no report on it is available and much valuable information has been lost.

Man: A Course of Study[44] is an American social science programme which has been used in a systematic way in Ireland within the City of Dublin Humanities Curriculum since 1973. The course combines the work of anthropologists with the theory of learning of Jerome Bruner. Bruner has outlined its aim as follows:

> The content of the course is man: his nature as a species, the forces that shaped and continue to shape his humanity.
> Three questions recur throughout:
> What is human about human beings?
> How did they get that way?
> How can they be made more so?
> We seek exercises and materials through which our pupils can learn wherein man is distinctive in his adaptation to the world and wherein there is a discernible continuity between him and his animal forbears.

Finally, there has been a growing interest in reviewing in part[45] or in whole the curriculum which is offered to pupils. A recent booklet entitled *The Extra Year: Enrichment in the School Curriculum*[46] suggests a series of steps by which a school may review its curriculum and establish its own priorities for development. Formative work in curriculum review and planning has been carried out and published by various vocational education committees.[47]

THE INFLUENCE OF EXAMINATIONS AND ASSESSMENT PROCEDURES ON THE CURRICULUM

Examinations and assessment procedures have always had a large influence on what is taught and how it is taught. In its policy statement *Establishing Priorities in the Curriculum* the IACD recognises that assessment is an integral part of the post-primary school system:

— it is an important component of school programmes
— it provides a terminal point which motivates some students
— it can provide teachers with the information needed to improve the curriculum
— it provides some information on performance for students, teachers and parents.

However, on account of the inflexible and subject-centred nature of the programmes to be assessed, the present public examination system is educationally unsatisfactory. If the curriculum is to cater for the needs of all students and to be responsive to the needs of society, then new, apt assessment procedures not limited to academic confines should be developed. The IACD believes that these new and varied modes of assessment must take account of the non-cognitive goals of education. Teachers should be involved in the development of these assessment procedures and have access to the various methods of assessment, together with inservice training in their application.

During the period, three influences on the public examination system as it affects the curriculum can be traced. First, there is the influence from the curriculum development projects which have been described earlier in this chapter. Some of the projects have developed alternative assessment procedures which have been accepted by the Department of Education in place of the equivalent public examinations at Intermediate or at Group Certificate level. The City of Dublin Humanities Curriculum has been accepted as the equivalent of English, History and Geography at both Intermediate and Group Certificate level each year since 1976. ISCIP has been accepted as the equivalent of Science Syllabus A over the same period. The Social and Environmental Studies Project has been accepted as the equivalent of History and Geography at Intermediate Certificate level each year since 1977. The alternative examination for Nua Chúrsa Gaeilge was accepted as the equivalent of the Irish paper at Intermediate Certificate level in 1978. In all these projects the teachers have built up skills in developing and implementing new assessment procedures involving project work, continuous assessment, and alternative, innovative styles of examination. In addition, there have been other courses which, although not accepted as the equivalent of public examinations, have also helped teachers build up and implement new skills in assessment. Pre-employment courses, career foundation courses, community-based learning within the SPIRAL Project, the junior cycle school certificate within the Early School-Leavers Project and the alternative mathematics course of North Tipperary VEC are all examples of projects in this category.

Secondly, there is the influence of reports on the public examination system. There has been the Madaus and MacNamara report on the Leaving Certificate entitled *Public Examinations*[48] and the final report of the committee on the form and function of the Intermediate Certificate examination, the *ICE Report*.[49] The ICE Report can be summarised in two statements made by the committee:

Some form of nationwide assessment at fifteen is needed for the sake of:

— feedback of norms to pupils, teachers and parents
— impartiality of an accepted sort
— guidance for further studies
— motivation to learning.

But such assessment needs to be:

— more varied in its modes the Intermediate Certificate examination so as to include assessment of oral, practical and project work, and to relate the mode of assessment to the objectives of the course that preceded it
— wider in its scope, reaching both higher and lower ranges of ability than the Intermediate Certificate examination grades
— broader in its objects, assessing both cognitive and non-cognitive factors
— more flexible, allowing for various forms of curriculum development and innovation
— frequent, occurring on more than a single occasion in junior cycle
— school-based, involving the teachers of the students concerned.

The committee proposed a system of school-based assessment monitored by a central body which would take responsibility for all aspects of assessing the curriculum, helping teachers to clarify educational objectives, providing external tests and opportunities for internal (school-based) assessments, and training teachers in the techniques and principles of assessment in curriculum development. It also recommended that all school-leavers should be given a certificate by the school, with information on all assessment, whether by external or internal tests.

It envisaged, too, that the monitoring or moderating of school-based assessment would be affected by collaboration between schools in small groupings. The ICE committee also established its own research project — the Public Examinations Evaluation Project (PEEP) — which began before the report was completed and continued in a full-time capacity until 1977 and after that in a part-time capacity until 1980.[50]

Thirdly, there is the influence of PEEP. In this project teachers were trained in the design of examinations and assessment procedures. They then devised multi-objective examinations in history and mathematics which were tried out on their pupils. In history, knowledge and comprehension were examined in addition to the higher order skills of evaluation of sources, logical argument in the presentation of the narrative and skills involved in the comprehension of data. Pupils also submitted projects (personal topics) which tested a variety of skills. In mathematics the teachers designed papers to test manipulative skills, application and analysis.

The final report of the project suggests the need for three levels of examination at Intermediate Certificate level. The first would correspond to the present higher level and the second to the present ordinary level. The third would meet the need of weaker pupils and would derive from a substantially different programme designed to help such pupils achieve mastery in basic skills. The report suggests that a certificate of competency would be awarded for such mastery. The investigations and experiments carried out by the team highlight the value of the computer in both the administration and analysis of examinations. They also suggest it would be possible to introduce a system of examination and moderation in which the teachers working in consortia are the first markers of their pupils' scripts.

The report differs from the ICE Report in that it places a far greater emphasis on a public examination component of assessment, suggests a more flexible approach to public examining is desirable and shows moderation to be a more complex problem than the ICE committee had thought.

Finally, it emphasisess the inter-connection between the curriculum and the public examination system:

> All these experiments demonstrate quite clearly that it is not possible to design examination and assessment procedures to test for higher

level skills, independently of participating in the design of the syllabus and suitable materials for training in these skills. The syllabus is the outcome of a complex design in which aims and objectives determine not only examining strategies, but teaching strategies as well. Multiple objective assessment strategies demand considerable changes in approach to teaching and learning which have considerable consequences for the construction of the syllabus.

SUMMARY

For the purpose of the enquiry, the curriculum is considered as consisting of all the planned educational experiences provided by the school to assist students in achieving specified aims or objectives. Curriculum development is the applied side of this definition. Its object is the improvement of programmes in educational institutions by changes in educational plans, teaching and learning. Since the 1960's, there has been a number of significant developments in education. Many have to do with the school organisation, structures, and the control of the new comprehensive and community schools. Others have occurred in school programmes. In this chapter, a number of major influences on the curriculum have been identified, and the responses and initiatives undertaken have been described.

A concern for the equality of educational opportunity was met by the widening of the Leaving Certificate programme in the late '60's to include a number of entirely new subjects.

Demographic changes as a result of free education and the raising of the school-leaving age, the introduction of a new curriculum in primary schools and a new interest in examination reform, led to a number of pilot experiments in curriculum development at junior cycle level in the early '70's. These included the Integrated Science (ISCIP), Humanities and Outdoor Education projects of the CDVEC Curriculum Development Unit located in Trinity College, Dublin; the Social and Environmental Studies Project based in the Curriculum Development Centre in St Patrick's Comprehensive School, Shannon, and the Irish Studies and Nua Chúrsa Gaeilge projects sponsored by the Department of Education.

The necessity for schools to be aware of industrial needs and manpower planning led to the introduction of pre-employment courses and to Ireland's participation in a network of projects on the theme of transition from school to adult/working life, sponsored by the Commission of the European Communities. These projects were called SPIRAL, Education for Development, and the Early School-Leavers Project, and were located in

Shannon, North Mayo and Dublin. In 1983, a second network of projects was initiated on a European basis and three of these projects were located in Shannon, Galway and Dublin.

A number of curriculum responses which emphasise personal development were also identified. These were developed to create a better balance in the curriculum. These programmes — transition year, pastoral care and social and health education were described.

The influence of the Council of Europe and the Modern Languages Projects developed at the Institiúid Teangeolaíochta Eireann and three new Irish projects were then described.

Other recent developments to expand and diversify the curriculum have included media studies, development education, projects in English and History as well as other projects initiated by individual schools or by groups of schools.

Finally, there has been the influence of public examinations and assessment procedures on the curriculum. Several of the curriculum projects described in this chapter have developed alternative assessment procedures which have been accepted by the Department of Education as the equivalent of public examinations. There has also been the work of PEEP.

2.

RESEARCH PROCEDURES

A survey of all post-primary principals was conducted by postal questionnaire in the spring of 1982. We surveyed the principals for a number of reasons. Principals have a role which allows them to act as the chief 'gate keepers' through which all innovations must pass. Principals are, arguably, in the best position to know what curriculum developments are being implemented in their schools. Principals also make curriculum decisions about the deployment of resources and are responsible for coordinating subject departments, relationship systems and activities such as inter-school liaison, relations with the Department of Education and, of course, internal staff and pupil relationships.

We felt we should avail ourselves of the opportunity to find out, too, the organisational arrangements within schools, sources of teacher support and constraint, and what developments principals wished to see.

AIMS OF THE SURVEY

To find out:
1   the extent and impact of curriculum development projects sponsored by the Department of Education, by curriculum development centres and by teachers at school level
2   what curriculum changes principals thought desirable
3   the main sources of teacher support in curriculum development
4   the main constraints on implementing curriculum changes in schools
5   modes of curriculum organisation; participation of pupils in public examinations; modes of grouping pupils for instruction; pupil transfer arrangements; alignment of curricula; and provision for remedial, guidance and physical education
6   the background and demographic data related to respondents and schools.

PRELIMINARY RESEARCH ACTIVITIES

Interviews

Several principals were interviewed to establish key issues and concepts relating to curriculum change in their respective schools. Every opportunity was allowed for freedom of response to designated interview 'probes' such as (a) impact of established curriculum projects, (b) perceived support structures for curriculum development and (c) problems and constraints facing schools.

Pilot Questionnaire

A pilot questionnaire containing four sections with 55 items was constructed. This draft of the questionnaire was subjected to the critical scrutiny of a wide range of groups and experts. It was discussed by the executive committee of the IACD and revised. It was discussed in detail with officers of the Department of Education at a special meeting relating to the survey. It was discussed at a research seminar in the Education Department, University College, Dublin. It was then redrafted and piloted in ten post-primary schools representing all types of schools and management structures, including schools in rural and urban areas. Critical comment was received from nine principals on substantive items, layout etc. This stage was considered a crucial test of acceptability. A third draft of the questionnaire was submitted to the Director of the Educational Research Centre, St Patrick's College, Drumcondra and was revised according to his comments. On the basis of this pilot work, the questionnaire was finalised.

METHOD

The Population

The respondents consisted of 505 principals representing all types of post-primary schools in the Republic of Ireland. The achieved population (N = 505) was 62% of the universe population (N = 815) of post-primary schools in the country. Table 2.1 sets out the target and achieved population figures by school-type in the survey.

Controlling for school type, 63% of all post-primary schools are secondary, 28% are vocational and 9% are community/comprehensive. Table 2.1 indicates that of the respondents (as a percentage of all survey respondents) 63% were from secondary schools, 28% from vocational schools and 9% from community/comprehensive schools.

Procedures

The questionnaire (see Appendix) was posted out in February 1982 and reminders were sent to non-respondents in March and May 1982. It

Table 2.1

TARGET AND ACHIEVED POPULATION OF SCHOOLS

	Secondary	Comprehensive	Community	Vocational	Total
Target population	524	14	35	242	815
Achieved population	318	12	32	143	505
Response rate	60.0	85.0	91.0	59.0	62

consisted of an introduction which set out the purposes of the project together with instructions for completing the five sections (which contained 78 items). Section 1, 'curriculum development in recent years', consisted of fifteen items requesting data on the impact and take-up of new courses at national level (pre-employment courses and applied Leaving Certificate courses); on the extent and nature of school-based curriculum development; and on familiarity, awareness and usage of formal curriculum development projects.

Section 2, 'desired curriculum changes/innovations in the future', consisted of twenty-one items seeking to ascertain the principals' views on desired change in the curriculum, their attitudes towards factors regarded as important sources of teacher support, and towards inservice education and training.

Section 3, 'constraints on curriculum development', consisted of fourteen items designed to gather evidence related to the constraints on successful curriculum development.

Section 4, 'organisational arrangements', consisted of twenty-one items designed to collect data relating to pupil transfer procedures; alignment of curricula; modes of grouping pupils for instruction; participation in public examinations; provision of guidance, remedial and physical education.

Section 5, 'background and demographic information', consisted of seven items and requested details of the respondent's age and sex as well as data related to the type of school, school size, geographic location, number of staff in school management. It was stressed that such information would be treated in total confidence and was essential for the overall analysis because it allowed school and principal characteristics to be related to dependent variables.

MODES OF ANALYSIS

Processing the Data

Each questionnaire contained a large number of items that were precoded. Only simple transformations were required to code open-ended response items. Procedures were set up whereby a complete check was made on all coding. A series of practice coding sessions was held to ensure unanimity among coders on the meaning of responses.

The data collected was then coded for analysis, checked and punched on IBM cards for tabulation. The data was analysed in accordance with procedures contained in the statistical package for the social sciences (SPSS)[1]

The data from the survey are presented in a number of different ways. In some cases, especially for the open-ended questions, simple frequency distributions of the responses to the questions are given. More commonly, however, crossclassifications of the data by response category and by school-type — whether secondary, vocational, community or comprehensive — are presented.

However, the interpretation of the tables does present some problems, arising mainly from non-response of one kind or another. There are two quite distinct types of non-response to the questions. First, there were 505 respondents (62%) from the 815 school principals. Secondly, even among respondents, some principals failed to answer all the questions asked. In a small number of cases as many as one hundred or one-hundred-and-fifty principals failed to answer a particular question, increasing overall non-response considerably.

There are two extreme assumptions that can be made about non-response in this or any similar type of survey:

(a)   the non-respondents share exactly the characteristics of the respondents: i.e. the respondents form a representative sample of the total population

(b)   the non-respondents differ markedly from the rest of the population.

Now, if the first assumption can be taken as reasonable then the figures emerging from the survey can be taken as characterising the population as a whole, with the sampling error calculated by standard statistical methods. In the present instance, it can be shown, if this assumption holds, that the ninety-five per cent limits would be of the order of three per cent. However, the sample itself cannot tell anything directly about the characteristics of the non-respondents, and if the first assumption is violated to a marked degree, then the overall characteristics of the population will differ from the sample characteristics by five to ten per cent — considerably more than the sampling error proper.

There are two indications that it is reasonable to assume that the sample is representative of the population. First, it can be shown that the number of pupils in each school-type for the responding schools corresponds to the number expected — i.e. the average school size is the same for respondents and non-respondents alike. Secondly, as mentioned in chapter one, the proportion of responding schools engaged in some type of curricular activity corresponds to the proportion in all schools.

Thus, in cases where there is a complete or almost complete set of answers to the survey questions, the assumption is made that the sample can be taken as broadly representative of the total population of schools. There was a somewhat higher response rate from the small number of community and comprehensive schools than from vocational and from secondary schools, and to remove the effect of over-representation — small though it is — from the results, the weighting system in Table 2.2 is used.

It is not possible to deal in the same way with the second type of non-response — the failure of principals to answer particular questions. The assumption that non-respondents share the same characteristics as respondents for this group is much more dubious — very often here non-response is likely to mean a negative response. Attention will be drawn to this where relevant in the text. Figures given in tables where more than fifty principals or so did not respond can only be taken as applying to the population as a whole if it is borne in mind that the true population figures could differ considerably from those in the sample. Overall figures in these cases are directly a summary of the respondents' position, and only indirectly can be applied to the population as a whole.

Table 2.2

WEIGHTING OF POPULATION BY TYPE OF SCHOOL			
Population	Target Population	Achieved Population	Weight Factor
Secondary	N = 524	N = 318	1.65
Vocational	N = 242	N = 143	1.69
Community	N = 35	N = 32	1.09
Comprehensive	N = 14	N = 12	1.17

CHARACTERISTICS OF THE SCHOOLS

The Independent Variables

Seven independent background variables were employed as controls in the study:

1   type of school and gender of school population
2   size of school
3   location of school
4   number of teachers
5   sex of respondent
6   school management (religious/lay)
7   age of respondent.

Type of School and Gender of School Population
For the purpose of reporting results, type of school was considered the most
important variable in crosstabulation with the dependent variables and
thus the results are generally reported with reference to it. Analysis was also
conducted with several other variables. Size of school and location were
considered the most important.

Table 2.3 shows the data related to the gender composition of the post-
primary school population which was obtained from 501 of the 505 schools
in this study. Fifty per cent of the schools in the survey are co-educational.
Of the remaining schools, 23% are boys' schools, 27% girls' schools. The
majority of comprehensive, community and vocational schools are co-
educational.

Table 2.3

GENDER CATEGORY BY TYPE OF SCHOOL

Gender Category	Secondary (N = 317)* %	Comprehensive (N = 12) %	Community (N = 31) %	Vocational (N = 141) %	All Schools %
Boys	33.8	8.3	3.2	4.3	22.9
Girls	41.6	16.7	0.0	2.1	27.3
Co-educational	24.6	75.0	96.8	93.6	49.8

*In the tables throughout the text, apart from Table 2.2, N gives the useable response for the
category of question.

Size of School
School size was considered to be of great importance in explaining
curriculum patterns. Throughout the report, schools are categorised as
either:

Small   having between 1 and 250 pupils
Medium   having between 251 and 600 pupils
Large   having more than 600 pupils.

Certain dependent variables were singled out for analysis by size of school. Of the 503 schools responding to this question, 30% have been categorised as small; 57% as medium and 13% as large. Table 2.4 sets out these data on school size by type of school.

Table 2.4

SIZE BY TYPE OF SCHOOL

Size	Secondary (N = 318) %	Comprehensive (N = 12) %	Community (N = 32) %	Vocational (N = 141) %	All Schools %
Small	22.6	8.3	9.4	50.4	30.0
Medium	66.0	58.3	37.5	40.4	57.2
Large	11.4	33.3	53.1	9.2	12.9

The majority of secondary and comprehensive schools are medium. The majority of community schools are large. Fifty per cent of vocational schools are small and most of the others are medium.

Location of School
Schools were classified as 'urban' if they were located in a city or town with a population of 5,000 or more and 'rural' if otherwise.

In all, 502 useable responses were coded for computer analysis. Table 2.5 sets out the location of schools by school type. Fifty-three per cent of the schools are classified as urban and 47% as rural. The majority of secondary and community schools are urban. The majority of vocational schools are rural.

Table 2.5

LOCATION BY TYPE OF SCHOOL

Location	Secondary (N = 317) %	Comprehensive (N = 12) %	Community (N = 32) %	Vocational (N = 141) %	All Schools %
Rural	40.7	50.0	43.8	61.7	47.0
Urban	59.3	50.0	56.3	38.3	53.0

Table 2.6 gives the population estimates relating to both size and location

and type of school. Most small schools are located in rural areas and most large schools are located in urban areas. Many small vocational schools are located in rural areas, while the majority of large comprehensive and community schools are located in urban areas. In both rural and urban areas the majority of secondary schools are medium.

Table 2.6

ESTIMATED NUMBERS OF SCHOOLS BY TYPE, SIZE AND LOCATION
Rural

Size	Secondary		Comprehensive		Community		Vocational		All Schools	
	Rural	Urban	Rural	Urban	Rural	Urban	Rural	Urban	Rural	Urban
Small	79	40	1	—	1	2	103	19	184	61
Medium	129	217	6	2	10	3	45	53	190	275
Large	5	54	—	5	4	15	2	20	11	94
Total	213	311	7	7	15	20	150	92	385	430

Number of Teachers
The number of full and part-time teachers was requested. The number of full-time teachers ranged from two teachers in one school to seventy-five teachers in the largest institution. The mean number of full-time staff was 23.1. When part-time staff were accounted for we found a range between sixty-two schools employing one part-time teacher and one school employing fifty-six part-time teachers. The mean number of part-time staff was 4.3.

Sex of Respondents
Data relating to the sex of respondents was collected from 498 principals (see Table 2.7). Sixty-one per cent of principals in this survey are male. However, in the secondary sector the majority are female. No doubt this is due to the large number of convent secondary schools in the system. In community and vocational schools more than 90% of the principals are male, while in comprehensive schools 83% are male. A recent enquiry in Northern Ireland[2] showed that 75% of post-primary principals were male.

School Management
Two enquiries were made regarding school management. First, we wished

Table 2.7

SEX OF RESPONDENTS BY TYPE OF SCHOOL

Sex of respondent	Secondary (N = 314) %	Comprehensive (N = 12) %	Community (N = 32) %	Vocational (N = 140) %	All Schools %
Female	57.0	16.7	6.3	5.7	39.0
Male	43.0	83.3	93.8	94.3	61.0

to determine if the school was under religious or lay management, and secondly, if religious management obtained, then what was the type: nuns, priests or brothers; or if lay management obtained, whether the type was vocational committee, management board, governors or other.

Replies to this question were received from 496 principals. Table 2.8 contains the data relating to management structure analysed by school type. Given the denominational nature of secondary schools, it is not surprising to find that religious management is dominant in those schools. Among schools with religious management, we find that 22% are managed by brothers, 16% by priests and 62% by nuns.

Comprehensive, community and vocational schools are overwhelmingly under lay management, although it is recognised that in many cases the boards are constituted on the basis of a partnership of lay and religious interests.

When lay management is examined, we find 67% are under vocational education committee structures, 21% are under a management board, 6% are managed by governors and 6% have some other form of management.

Table 2.8

FORM OF MANAGEMENT BY TYPE OF SCHOOL

Form of Management	Secondary (N = 315) %	Comprehensive (N = 12) %	Community (N = 31) %	Vocational (N = 138) %	All Schools %
Religious	91.7	8.3	0.0	0.0	59.1
Lay	8.3	91.7	100.0	100.0	40.9

Age of Principals

Finally, we examined the age pattern of respondents. In all 495 principals replied to this question. The modal age for respondents was 41 - 50 years of age with 42% falling into this category. Three principals were between 25 and 30 years of age. With the exception of comprehensive schools, there is a very similar age pattern among principals when analysed by type of school. The data is given in Table 2.9.

Table 2.9

AGE OF RESPONDENTS BY TYPE OF SCHOOL

Age	Secondary (N = 313) %	Comprehensive (N = 12) %	Community (N = 32) %	Vocational (N = 138) %	All Schools %
25 - 30	0.6	0.0	0.0	0.7	0.6
31 - 40	30.0	8.3	28.1	28.3	29.1
41 - 50	41.5	50.0	50.0	42.0	42.2
51 - 60	24.3	41.7	21.9	23.2	24.1
61 +	3.5	0.0	0.0	5.8	4.0

SUMMARY

A five-part questionnaire concerning curriculum development was circulated to all post-primary principals in the Irish Republic during the spring term 1982. The achieved response rate was 62% (N = 505). Comprehensive and community schools were heavily represented in the returns with about three-fifths of secondary and vocational schools represented.

About half the schools are co-educational and medium in size with a pupil enrolment of between 250 - 600. Fifty-three per cent were urban and 47% rural. Sixty-one per cent of respondents were male and 59% were from religious managed schools. Forty-two per cent were between 41 and 50 years of age.

3.

PRINCIPALS' VIEWS ON
CURRICULUM DEVELOPMENT 1970-1982

Three ways of developing curricula have been identified: first, the central development model nationally funded and emanating from the Department of Education; second, the school-based model emanating from individual schools; third, the formal pilot curriculum development project emanating from a group of schools but coordinated and often funded from an agency outside the schools.

The central development model is described first. Three kinds of courses conforming to this model have been identified: pre-employment courses, new Leaving Certificate courses, and some courses or modules of courses which are available to all schools.

PRE-EMPLOYMENT COURSES (PEC)

Principals were asked:

— Does your school offer a pre-employment course?
— Has your school offered this course in the past?
— In what year was the pre-employment course first introduced in your school?
— If your school does not offer a pre-employment course, would your school like to offer such a course?

Extent of Provision
Table 3.1 indicates provision of pre-employment courses by school type and size in the year of the survey. In all, some 45% of schools eligible to provide these courses did so. The data suggests that provision of PEC is highly related to school size. While 67% of large schools and 59% of medium schools offered PEC , only 24% of small schools did so. PEC is offered in 40% of comprehensive schools, 59% in community and 43% of vocational schools.

Table 3.1

PERCENTAGE OF SCHOOLS WHICH CURRENTLY OFFER
PRE-EMPLOYMENT COURSES BY SCHOOL TYPE AND SIZE
(Excluding Secondary Schools)*

	Comprehensive (N = 10) %	Community (N = 32) %	Vocational (N = 141) %	All Schools %
Small	—	—	25.4	24.4
Medium	42.9	50.0	61.4	58.8
Large	50.0	76.5	61.5	67.4
Total	40.0	59.4	43.3	45.1

*At the time of the survey secondary schools were precluded from offering PEC. Secondary schools are excluded from Tables 3.1 and 3.2

It should be noted that secondary schools were precluded from offering PEC at the time of the survey. This was due to the European Social Fund rules governing the funding of these courses. The situation has now changed.

In response to the next question 'has your school offered this course in the past?' The percentage of schools (omitting secondary schools) which replied 'yes' (see Table 3.2) was 59.9% — 14.8% more than the number currently offering PEC. This difference may reflect the way pre-employment courses respond to local needs and depend on the number of students who apply for them. Thus, while the number of courses offered in any one recent year may not have exceeded 45% of the comprehensive, community and vocational schools which offered them in the year of the survey, the number of schools which have offered these courses in one or more years is 60% of the total number of eligible schools.

Comparison of the number of pre-employment courses offered in the year of the survey with the number of courses offered in the past shows the importance of school size as a factor in determining whether a school can provide a pre-employment course and also whether it can continue to provide such a course each year.

Sixty-seven per cent of large schools offered the course as compared with 59% of medium schools and 24% of small schools (Table 3.1). Further analysis shows that the percentage of large and medium schools which offered the course in the year of the survey as compared with those which have ever offered it only dropped by 6-9%, whereas the percentage of small schools dropped by 23%.

Table 3.2

PERCENTAGE OF SCHOOLS WHICH HAVE OFFERED
PRE-EMPLOYMENT COURSES BY SCHOOL TYPE AND SIZE
(Excluding Secondary Schools)

	Comprehensive (N = 9) %	Community (N = 31) %	Vocational (N = 139) %	All* Schools %
Small	0.0	0.0	49.1	47.5
Medium	71.4	58.3	68.4	68.1
Large	50.0	82.3	69.2	73.1
Total	54.5	64.7	59.1	59.9

*See note to Table 3.1. There were 179 useable responses to this question of a possible 185.

When the location of schools was considered, we find that 36% of rural and 59% of urban schools made provision for pre-employment courses in the year of the survey. Further analysis indicates that 71% of urban and 52% of rural schools have provided for pre-employment courses at some time in the past.

Rate of Implementation
Principals were asked in what year the pre-employment course was introduced into their school. Their replies give some indication of the rate of implementation of new courses. Sixteen per cent of principals said they had introduced the course prior to 1977, the year of its formal introduction by the Department of Education. Fifty-one per cent said that they had introduced it in 1977 or 1978, 26% in 1979 or 1980 and 7% since 1981. The pattern of responses indicates the small number of schools which offered such courses prior to 1977 and which were presumably one of the influences on the Department of Education when guidelines were being drawn up for pre-employment courses. Then with the publication of the guidelines and sanction for the courses in 1977 there was a rapid increase in the number of schools which offered the courses in the first two years, followed by a more gradual increase in the next two years, and an even smaller number of new schools introducing the course since 1981.

Interest in the Future
The final question in relation to pre-employment courses was aimed at determining the amount of interest in offering this course in the future by

schools which had not so far offered the course. Table 3.3 shows that 67 % of the schools which answered this question said they would like to offer such a course. When these replies were analysed, controlling for location of school it was found that almost 72 % of schools in rural areas and 43 % of schools in urban areas would like to offer the course in the future. (If it were assumed that all the thirty-seven non-respondents to this question were not interested in introducing the course, these percentages would be some seven to eight points lower.)

Table 3.3

PERCENTAGE OF SCHOOLS INTERESTED IN INTRODUCING
PRE-EMPLOYMENT COURSES IN FUTURE

	Secondary (N = 277) %	Comprehensive (N = 5) %	Community (N = 13) %	Vocational (N = 75) %	All* Schools %
Yes	64.3	60.0	76.9	77.3	67.3
No	35.7	40.0	23.1	22.7	32.7

*Useable responses were obtained from 370 of a possible 407 schools.

This interest in pre-employment courses may spring from the need for pupils to secure vocational skills at a time of increasing economic recession and unemployment. It may also be a measure of the failure of the present Leaving Certificate to meet the needs of all the pupils who stay in school after Junior Cycle.

NEW LEAVING CERTIFICATE COURSES

A major influence on the curriculum has been the concern for equality of educational opportunity.[1] One of the most significant means of achieving this has been the introduction in 1969 of a number of new subjects at Leaving Certificate level. In the survey principals were given a list of these new subjects and asked if their school currently taught the subjects and if so, in what year they were introduced. The responses to this question varied from 319 to 452 of the possible 505 replies. An examination of non-response indicated that, in general, the majority of those not responding corresponded to school types with least involvement and would probably have given negative responses. The discussion which follows is in terms of actual respondents. Inclusion of non-respondents as negative would lower overall percentages by one or two points while leaving the pattern which is discussed unchanged.

Extent of Provision

Table 3.4 shows the percentage of schools which provide these courses and the percentage of schools providing them analysed by type of school. Of the Leaving Certificate courses mentioned in the survey, accountancy and business organisation are listed as being provided by over 80% of schools while economic history, agricultural economics and mechanics are availed of least by schools. The pattern of provision varies significantly when analysed by type of school: comprehensive, community and vocational schools offer a much wider choice. With the exceptions of economic history, agricultural economics and mechanics all the subjects are well provided for in these schools. The most striking difference between provision in these schools and secondary schools is in technical drawing, engineering, workshop theory and practice and building construction. The only new subjects to be provided in more than 50% of the secondary schools are accountancy, business organisation, home economics (social and scientific/general) and economics.

The number of schools which currently provide these Leaving Certificate subjects was analysed by size of school to determine whether the number of pupils in a school affected provision. The results are contained in Table 3.5. The same pattern is apparent as in pre-employment courses. Large schools are more likely to offer a wider range of courses than small schools. This is true of most of the courses analysed. However, the difference is greater in accountancy, business organisation and economics than in technical drawing, engineering, workshop theory and practice and building construction. In these latter three subjects the number of small schools which provide the courses is greater than the number of medium schools. The likely explanation of this is that almost all vocational schools which offer a Leaving Certificate course include these subjects and 50% of vocational schools are small.

One of the major aspirations of Dr Hillery's plan which was discussed in Chapter One was to improve the curriculum, particularly of schools in remote rural areas by providing these new Leaving Certificate courses. In Table 3.6 provision is analysed by the location of the school. Of the subjects introduced in 1969, no significant differences between urban and rural schools were found in the provision of economic history, accountancy, business organisation and home economics (general) and mechanics. It should be stressed that economic history and mechanics have not made impact in schools as less than 2% of schools offered mechanics and 15% offered economic history. While differences were not found between urban

Table 3.4

PERCENTAGES OF SCHOOLS WHICH PROVIDE
NEW LEAVING CERTIFICATE COURSES BY TYPE

Subject	Number* of Responses	Sec. %	Comp. %	Comm. %	Voc. %	All Schools* %
Technical drawing	(N = 444)	35.1	91.7	96.8	93.4	57.9
Economic history	(N = 356)	15.7	40.0	17.6	7.4	14.3
Engineering workshop theory and practice	(N = 408)	4.5	90.9	89.3	81.7	35.2
Building construction	(N = 414)	14.5	90.9	92.9	82.7	41.5
Accountancy	(N = 450)	79.3	90.9	96.6	82.9	81.2
Business organisation	(N = 452)	80.1	81.8	96.6	86.1	82.5
Home economics (scientific and social)	(N = 427)	67.4	90.0	93.1	67.0	68.8
Home economics (general)	(N = 406)	51.5	70.0	82.6	71.0	58.4
Agricultural economics	(N = 339)	5.6	20.0	6.3	12.3	7.6
Economics	(N = 411)	66.0	72.7	81.5	57.1	64.7
Mechanics	(N = 319)	0.4	12.3	15.3	1.3	1.3

*See page 51 dealing with these new courses.

and rural schools, subjects such as accountancy and business organisation were provided by over 80% of schools to Leaving Certificate level. Around 63% or rural schools and 54% of urban schools offer home economics (general).

Rural schools make significantly greater provision for technical drawing, engineering, workshop theory and practice, building construct- ion, home economics (scientific and social) and agricultural economics. The probable explanation of this is that half of the vocational schools are rural and these schools are more likely to offer these subjects. Economics, which is offered by 70% of urban schools as opposed to 59% of rural schools, is the only subject in which there is significantly greater provision in urban than rural schools. These findings go a long way towards affirming that Dr Hillery's proposals for technical education in rural areas have proved successful.

Table 3.5

PERCENTAGE OF SCHOOLS PROVIDING
NEW LEAVING CERTIFICATE COURSES BY SIZE

Subjects	Number of responses*	Small %	Medium %	Large %	All Schools %
Technical drawing	(N = 444)	58.9	56.1	63.2	57.9
Economic history	(N = 356)	12.3	14.6	17.6	14.3
Engineering workshop theory and practice	(N = 408)	40.1	29.7	47.5	35.2
Building construction	(N = 414)	47.6	35.7	52.1	41.5
Accountancy	(N = 450)	63.3	86.0	93.4	81.2
Business organisation	(N = 452)	69.9	84.7	97.2	82.5
Home economics (scientific and social)	(N = 427)	57.9	70.9	83.3	68.8
Home economics (general)	(N = 407)	56.2	57.5	67.4	58.4
Agriculural economics	(N = 339)	6.5	8.8	4.6	7.6
Economics	(N = 411)	48.5	67.4	84.0	64.7
Mechanics	(N = 319)	0.0	1.3	4.1	1.3

*See note to Table 3.4.

Table 3.6

PERCENTAGE OF SCHOOLS PROVIDING
NEW LEAVING CERTIFICATE COURSES BY LOCATION

Subjects	Number of Responses*	Rural %	Urban %	All Schools %
Technical drawing	(N = 444)	68.3	48.0	57.9
Economic history	(N = 356)	14.1	14.6	14.3
Engineering workshop theory and practice	(N = 408)	43.0	28.2	35.2
Building construction	(N = 414)	52.0	31.8	41.5
Accountancy	(N = 450)	79.7	83.6	81.2
Business organisation	(N = 452)	82.4	82.4	82.5
Home economics (scientific and social)	(N = 427)	73.7	64.1	68.8
Home economics (general)	(N = 407)	62.7	54.4	58.4
Agricultural economics	(N = 399)	12.1	3.8	7.6
Economics	(N = 411)	58.8	69.8	64.7
Mechanics	(N = 319)	0.9	1.7	1.3

*See note to Table 3.4

The Rate of Implementation

Principals were also asked to state the year in which they introduced these new courses to their schools (Table 3.7). As can be seen, the response rates to this question were disappointingly low. However, the analysis of the available replies showed that the same type of pattern as was described for pre-employment courses is, in general, apparent. More than 30% of schools which offer a subject have tended to introduce it within the first three years of its being available. In the case of technical drawing, engineering workshop theory and practice and building construction, the number of new schools introducing the subject dropped over the next four-year period, but then rose again in the later 70's. In the case of most of the other subjects the number of schools introducing the subject remained

Table 3.7

PERCENTAGE OF SCHOOLS WHICH INTRODUCED
NEW LEAVING CERTIFICATE COURSES BY YEAR*

Subject	Number of Responses	1971 or before	1972-75	1976-79	Since 1980 -
Technical drawing	(N = 233)	33.0	22.8	33.0	11.2
Economic history	(N = 47)	12.8	6.4	40.4	40.4
Engineering workshop theory and practice	(N = 137)	40.1	21.9	32.2	5.8
Building construction	(N = 156)	32.1	22.5	34.5	10.9
Accountancy	(N = 309)	43.7	24.6	24.4	6.3
Business organisation	(N = 318)	36.8	26.8	29.5	6.9
Home economics (scientific and social)	(N = 250)	18.4	17.6	50.8	13.2
Home economics (general)	(N = 199)	62.3	15.5	19.1	3.1
Agricultural economics	(N = 19)	26.3	15.8	42.1	15.8
Economics	(N = 217)	32.3	29.1	29.9	8.7
Mechanics	(N = 7)	28.6	28.6	28.6	14.2

*Based on responses for which dates were available.

approximately the same throughout the 1970's. In all cases, the number of schools introducing the subject dropped since 1980. Home economics (social and scientific) and home economics (general) were the only subjects which do not fit this pattern. The likely explanation in the case of the three technical subjects may be that in the later 70's there was greater provision of facilities and perhaps of teachers. In all cases, the drop in the number of new schools offering the subject since 1980 is in part accounted for by the smaller number of years included under this heading and perhaps in part by the fact that by 1980 the number of schools which wished to provide the subject were already doing so. Any conclusions from this data must be extremely tentative and they should be taken to show only the general pattern of the rate of implementation of new courses throughout the system.

OTHER COURSES OR MODULES OF COURSES

The Department of Education has introduced certain other courses or modules of courses since 1980 and principals were asked to name which of these were taught in their school. The data suggests that the computer module in mathematics is the most popular of these innovations. Of secondary schools responding (n = 205) 73% reported they had introduced the computer module; 56% of comprehensive schools (n = 9), 87% of community schools (n = 24) and 52% of vocational schools (n = 96) have implemented this curriculum change. Classical Studies was reported to be operating in 6% of the schools responding to the survey. Of the two modules of courses mentioned, by far the more popular is the computer module. This was found to operate in 72% of urban schools (n = 135) and 64% of rural ones (n = 103).

THE SCHOOL-BASED MODEL

School-based curriculum development is a new name for a very old idea. More than fifty years ago Alfred North Whitehead commented that the 'first requisite for educational reform is the school as a unit with its approved curriculum based on its own needs, and evolved by its own staff'.[2] School-based curriculum development was defined as any innovation originating at 'grassroots' level, whether in one school or in a group of schools, in the content of the curriculum, teaching strategies and methods, or in modes of pupil assessment and evaluation.

For the purpose of the survey school-based curriculum development which derived its impetus from the school and which normally depended on the efforts of the teachers of the school, perhaps with voluntary outside support such as from a consultant from a university or college or a teacher centre, was distinguished from curriculum development projects which, while also school-based, derived their impetus from funding by an agency outside the school.

Principals were asked whether they had taken part in any school-based curriculum development project or experimental training teaching scheme since 1970? If their answer to this question was yes they were asked to complete the following five items:

— name the scheme and add a brief description of it
— where did the scheme originate?
— is it supported by an outside agency and if so, please indicate the type of support
— are you or members of your staff using the scheme this year?
— have any other schools been involved in the project or scheme?

Extent

Two hundred and sixteen of the 483 schools responding to this question indicated that they had participated in some form of school-based curriculum development since 1970. Table 3.8 gives the percentage participating for each school type. The data indicates significant differences between types of schools in their involvement in school-based curriculum development. Comprehensive and community schools report very high levels of involvement in such activity whereas 45% of secondary and 33% of vocational principals reported involvement in local curricular initiatives during the past twelve years. The relatively low percentage of vocational schools participating in school-based curriculum development may be due to two factors — the exclusion of schools working with the CDVEC Curriculum Development Unit from this section of the survey and the exclusion of pre-employment courses which have been described above. The results generally indicate a very encouraging amount of activity of this nature in schools throughout the country.

Table 3.8

PARTICIPATION IN SCHOOL-BASED CURRICULUM DEVELOPMENT
(SBCD) SCHEMES BY SCHOOL TYPE SINCE 1970

	Secondary (N = 307) %	Comprehensive (N = 12) %	Community (N = 30) %	Vocational (N = 134) %	All Schools* %
Yes	44.6	91.3	80.0	32.8	43.5
No	55.4	8.7	20.0	67.2	56.5

*Useable responses were obtained from 483 of a possible 505 schools.

Principals' replies were then analysed by size and location (Table 3.9). Considerable differences on both these variables were found.

Sixty-eight per cent of large schools as opposed to 25% of small schools and 51% of urban schools as opposed to 35% of rural schools have been involved in some form of school-based curriculum development since 1970. One possible interpretation of this finding is that rural schools are still more traditional in their approach to the curriculum than urban schools. Alternatively, the fact that 62% of vocational schools had been classified as rural and many of these schools offer pre-employment courses may account for the lesser amount of school-based curriculum development in rural schools. With regard to size of school the same pattern is apparent as with both pre-employment courses and the new Leaving Certificate subjects, namely that large schools are more likely to provide a wider curriculum than small schools.

Table 3.9

PARTICIPATION IN SCHOOL-BASED CURRICULUM
DEVELOPMENT BY SCHOOL TYPE, SIZE AND LOCATION

	Sec-ondary		Compre-hensive		Comm--unity		Voc-ational		All *Schools	
	(N = 125) %	(N = 181)	(N = 6) %	(N = 6)	(N = 13) %	(N = 11)	(N = 83) %	(N = 51)	%	
	Rural	Urban	Rural	Urban	Rural	Urban	Rural	Urban	Rural	Urban
Small	30.4	41.7	0.0	—	100.0	100.0	15.8	100.0	22.9	36.1
Medium	46.1	45.2	100.0	100.0	75.0	50.0	28.0	63.3	46.5	49.4
Large	66.7	60.6	—	100.0	50.0	92.3	100.0	63.6	62.5	70.5
Total	40.8	47.5	83.3	100.0	69.2	88.2	20.5	52.9	35.0	51.4

* There were 482 useable responses received of the possible 505.

Type of Provision

The principals who reported an involvement in school-based curriculum development were also asked to indicate the type of innovation. These open questions were subsequently coded into nine categories and Table 3.10 gives the number of individual projects carried out by schools. Some schools offer more than one type of project and so the total number of projects (274) is higher than the 216 schools which have provided these projects. Secondary schools (n = 137) were involved in 174 separate curriculum development projects while comprehensive schools (n = 11) reported 15 such projects, community schools (n = 24) reported 32 projects and vocational schools (n = 44) reported 53 separate curriculum development projects at local level.

By far the most popular area for school-based decentralised curriculum development is the area of pastoral care. Ninety-two schools reported an involvement with pastoral care of one kind or another. Team teaching, health education and enrichment-type junior cycle programmes including integrated studies were also mentioned by thirty or more different schools.

Many principals answered this question in detail. A sample of their replies follows:

1   A large urban secondary school has a programme devised by the school in which a series of modules is offered and the students take these in turn. The modules include media studies, preparation for life, public speaking, child psychology, computers and budgeting. Team

Table 3.10

NUMBER AND TYPE OF SCHOOL-BASED
CURRICULUM DEVELOPMENT
PROJECTS BY SCHOOL TYPE

Projects	Secondary (N = 137)	Comprehensive (N = 11)	Community (N = 24)	Vocational (N = 44)	Total* (N = 216)
Pastoral care	60	3	12	17	92
Health education	21	2	4	3	30
Media studies/ communication	18	0	1	1	20
Foundation year	6	1	4	2	13
Special — remedial education	11	0	2	8	21
Enrichment-type junior cycle (integrated studies)	20	3	5	3	31
Social education	7	2	3	3	15
3-Year Leaving Certificate/ Extra Year/ Transition Year	10	1	0	3	14
Team teaching	21	3	1	13	38
Total	174	15	32	53	274

*Numbers represent projects being conducted in 216 schools.

teaching and role play form part of the programme and the emphasis is on the personal development of the students.

2   A large urban comprehensive school has a programme devised by the school which involves the following:

Creative Studies at first year level

(home economics, woodwork, metalwork, drama, music, art and mechanical drawing)
A three-year Integrated Studies Programme
(including English and social and environmental studies)
A special studies programme in a Transition Year
(media studies, drama, business operations, home care)
Special Studies
(personal development and discussion groups throughout the school).

3   A medium secondary school for boys in a rural area has an integrated studies course in English, history and geography for first year pupils which was devised by the teachers. Each class has the same teacher for all three subjects. The teachers meet for one class period each week to plan and monitor the course.

4   A large secondary school for girls in an urban area has a six-year cycle and uses first year as a transition year from primary to post-primary. The teachers, at the instigation of the remedial teacher, have evolved a special programme which includes integrated studies.

5   A medium co-educational secondary school in a rural area has a pastoral care system which was devised by the guidance counsellor and was used with all first and second year students.

6   A medium co-educational secondary school in a rural area has developed a new experimental teaching strategy which includes mixed-ability teaching. One half-day of the timetable has been restructured and is used for a personal development programme which includes an integrated approach, team teaching and planning.

7   A large secondary school for girls in an urban area has devised a foundation year for weak students. It has worked out its own pastoral care programme and integrated studies and has been involved with the Department of Education pilot programme called Nua Chúrsa Gaeilge.

Origins

The principals who had replied that they had a school-based curriculum development programme in their school were then asked where the scheme originated. Seventy-four per cent of those who responded said it originated with members of their own staff. The rest gave a variety of answers — Department of Education inservice courses, through subject associations, in other schools nearby, in a teachers' centre, in another country. It seems likely these other answers refer to the stimulus given to members of staff and that the almost universal answer to the question 'Where does school-based curriculum development schemes originate' is with members of the school staff.

External Support
Principals were also asked if they received support for these schemes from any outside agency. Sixty-four per cent of the respondents said they did not and 36% said they did. Among the agencies listed as supporting these schemes were: Department of Education inservice courses, teachers' centres, teacher training institutions, subject associations, VEC's, state-sponsored bodies, institutions such as the Irish Film Institute.

Current Provision
Principals were asked whether the school-based development project was still in operation in their school. Eighty-nine per cent replied that it was. The percentage of schools which have initiated such schemes and subsequently dropped them varies very little when classified by type or size of school. This finding is of particular importance with regard to size of school and the data is given in Table 3.11.

Table 3.11

CURRENT USE OF SCHOOL-BASED
CURRICULUM DEVELOPMENT SCHEME
CLASSIFIED BY SIZE OF SCHOOL

Size of School	Yes	No
Small (N = 32)	84.3	15.7
Medium (N = 115)	90.4	9.6
Large (N = 40)	87.5	12.5
Total	88.8	11.2

Eighty-four per cent of small schools, 90% of medium schools and 88% of large schools continue to offer the school-based scheme which originated in their school.

Teachers in schools of all sizes show they are able to sustain an innovation which they have begun. However, it must also be remembered that the percentage of small schools which offer a school-based course is low compared with the percentage of medium and large schools.

Dissemination
Principals were asked if any other schools were involved in the project or scheme. The results suggest a mixed situation regarding the interaction of

other schools in school-based curriculum development schemes. Roughly one-third of schools report outside involvement, one-third claim no outside involvement and one-third do not know if there is external cooperation or involvement.

Programmes for Children with Special Needs

Principals were also asked whether their school had a programme for children with special needs. Special needs were defined to include special programmes for handicapped pupils or pupils of exceptional ability. Almost 38% of principals replied that they had such a programme and when analysed by type of school the comprehensive and community schools are more likely to provide such special education programmes. When the principals' replies were analysed by size and location it was found that 63% of large schools provided some kind of special education programme whereas only 18% of small schools did so. Forty-two per cent of urban schools and 33% of rural schools provided these programmes.

Finally, principals were asked to describe the programme. By far the most frequently mentioned programme was remedial education through a withdrawal system from classes. Other programmes that were mentioned were for blind, deaf or physically handicapped pupils, special education programmes for mentally handicapped pupils, special programmes for exceptional/bright pupils and special programmes in aesthetic and music education.

FORMAL CURRICULUM DEVELOPMENT PROJECTS

These projects are also normally school-based, but they derive their impetus from an agency outside the school that provides funds. The agencies identified as sponsoring these projects were the Department of Education, the City of Dublin Vocational Education Committee's Curriculum Development Unit in Trinity College, the Curriculum Development Centre at Shannon, Institiúid Teangeolaíochta Éireann, the Health Education Bureau and the Irish Foundation for Human Development.

Familiarity

Principals were asked to indicate their level of familiarity with a number of formal curriculum projects on a specially devised scale ranging from 'I am unfamiliar with the project' (level 1) to 'I am currently involved with the project' (level 5). Their responses are summarised in Table 3.12. All the projects described are considered to be pilot experimental projects. While some have been fully evaluated, no decision has been made about their

Table 3.12

PRINCIPALS' FAMILIARISATION WITH
FORMAL CURRICULUM DEVELOPMENT PROJECTS

Project	Un-familiar (%)	Heard of Project (%)	Used Materials (%)	Been a Pilot School (%)	Cur-rently Involved (%)
City of Dublin Humanities (CDU)* (N = 460)**	32.8	55.7	8.1	0.5	2.9
Early School Leavers (CDU) (N = 431)	60.5	34.4	3.5	—	1.6
Education for Development (North Mayo) (N = 422)	64.7	31.8	1.9	1.2	0.5
Health Education (HEB) (N = 466)	8.9	42.9	37.5	2.9	7.8
Institiúid Teangeolaíochta Éireann (Modern Languages) (ITE) (N = 431)	40.4	45.4	10.2	1.2	2.9
Irish Studies (Department of Education) (N = 434)	33.1	57.3	8.1	1.1	0.4
Integrated Science ISCIP(CDU) (N = 436)	45.9	38.9	11.4	0.9	3.1
Nua Chúrsa Gaeilge (Department of Education) (N = 423)	33.9	50.0	12.6	3.0	1.0
Outdoor Education Project (CDU) (N = 420)	68.3	25.8	3.4	0.5	1.9
Social and Environmental Studies Project (SESP) (Shannon Curriculum Centre) (N = 444)	25.7	61.0	8.9	2.3	2.0
SPIRAL: Shannon Project of Interventions for relevant adolescent learnings (Shannon Curriculum Centre) (N = 438)	45.4	44.1	5.8	1.0	3.7
Transition Year (Department of Education) (N = 459)	7.3	78.9	9.0	1.5	3.3

*CDU is the CDVEC Curriculum Development Unit, Trinity College, Dublin.
**See comment on Response Rate prior to Table 3.4.

implementation or dissemination on a wider scale, and thus the percentage of schools which report they are currently involved with the project (column 5) is in every case very small.

Comparison between individual projects is very difficult as the projects vary on several major criteria. Some have been in existence since 1972 (City of Dublin Humanities, Social and Environmental Studies, ISCIP) while the most recent began in 1979 (the Early School-Leavers Project). Many operate in a local network of pilot schools (e.g. those connected with the CDVEC Curriculum Development Unit in Dublin or the Curriculum Development Centre in Shannon), while those sponsored by the Department of Education operate in pilot schools scattered throughout the country. Some projects are single subject (e.g. ISCIP, Nua Chúrsa Gaeilge), others cover several subjects (e.g. Irish Studies, Humanities and SESP) or the whole curriculum for a particular age group (e.g. the three transition from school to adult life projects — SPIRAL, Education for Development and Early School-Leavers).

In addition, some respondents interpreted health education and transition year more widely than was intended. Within health education was included the work of the regional health boards, and within transition year was included some transition programmes from primary to secondary school. Despite the blurring of categories in these two cases, transition year and health education are the two projects about which principals are by far the most aware. In each case, more than 90% of the principals have heard of these projects or use materials or ideas from them. Most other projects which have been in existence since the mid-1970's have been heard of by more than 65% of the principals. The exceptions are the Outdoor Education Project (32%) and ISCIP (54%). Of the most recent projects, SPIRAL and the Modern Languages projects have been heard of by more than 50% of the respondents.

Extent of Involvement

The survey identified three kinds of active involvement with the projects: use of materials or ideas from the projects, experience of having been a pilot school, and current involvement with a project.

When the three kinds of active involvement are amalgamated we find that 10%-17% (omitting Outdoor Education at 6% and Health Education at 49%) have participated in the longer established projects. It is of interest to note that Nua Chúrsa Gaeilge (17%), ISCIP (15%) and Modern Languages (14%), which all represent single discipline projects, have slightly higher percentages of involvement than the interdisciplinary projects. Thirteen per cent of schools had been involved with SESP, 12% with Humanities and 10% with Irish Studies.

The percentage of schools currently involved or which have been pilot schools (levels 4/5) is generally small. This is because of the experimental pilot nature of the projects and the corresponding restrictions on the number of schools allowed to participate.

In the case of the three interdisciplinary projects — SESP, Humanities and Irish Studies — the main thrust is very similar and there has been virtually no overlap in pilot schools (levels 4/5). Thus, we know that the number of schools involved as pilot schools or which are currently involved with these three projects is almost 10% of the total.

NUMBER OF SCHOOLS INVOLVED

It has been possible from the responses to the survey to find out how many schools have been involved in curriculum development of some kind since 1970. Since almost all schools offer the Leaving Certificate and include some of the new Leaving Certificate courses described earlier in this chapter, almost all schools have been involved in curriculum development. For this reason, in order to find out the number of schools involved in curriculum development outside the main stream of Group, Intermediate and Leaving Certificate, we have included only those schools participating in a pre-employment course, or in a school-based curriculum development project, or as a pilot school in one of the formal curriculum projects. Table 3.13 gives the percentage of schools participating in one or other of these three types of projects. Sixty-two per cent of the schools which responded to the survey are involved in one or more of the projects. Almost every comprehensive and community school has been involved, as have more than 75% of vocational schools and 50% of secondary schools. The smaller percentage of secondary schools participating in any form of curriculum development is probably accounted for by the fact that such schools have not in the past been allowed to offer pre-employment courses, or that in some cases the existing curriculum provision meets the needs of their student intake. It must also be borne in mind that 67% of school principals responding to the survey stated a wish to start a pre-employment course in their school.

The total of 62% of schools which have found it necessary to offer some alternative or addition to the Group, Intermediate or Leaving Certificate courses shows that these courses do not adequately fulfil the existing needs of the schools. It is also significant that so many schools have been able to provide alternative courses within the existing system. It was also possible to establish from the principals' replies how many of these alternative courses were offered by each of the schools. The number and percentage of schools which offer one, two or more than two alternative courses are given

Table 3.13

PERCENTAGE OF SCHOOLS PARTICIPATING IN
CURRICULUM DEVELOPMENT SINCE 1970

	Secondary N = 318	Comprehensive N = 12	Community N = 32	Vocational N = 143	All Schools N = 505
Participating in one or more projects	52.5	100.0	90.6	76.2	62.2
Not participating in any project	47.5	—	9.4	23.8	37.9

Table 3.14

NUMBER AND PERCENTAGE OF SCHOOLS WITH
CURRICULUM DEVELOPMENT PROJECTS BY TYPE OF SCHOOL

Project	Secondary N %	Comprehensive N %	Community N %	Vocational N %	All Schools %
1 or more	167 52.5	12 100.0	29 90.6	109 76.2	62.2
2 or more	47 14.8	8 66.7	18 56.3	32 22.4	18.4
3 or more	18 5.7	7 58.3	9 28.1	11 7.7	7.3
4 or more	6 1.9	1 8.3	9 24.9	9 6.3	4.3
5 or more	— —	— —	6 18.7	5 3.5	1.8

in Table 3.14. More than 18% of the schools offer two alternative courses and more than 7% offer three or more such courses. The majority of comprehensive and community schools offer at least two of these courses whereas some 15% of secondary schools and 22% of vocational schools offer at least two courses.

Finally, the table shows the number of schools which participate in 3, 4 or 5 or more of these alternative programmes. These may be considered the most innovative schools in the country. Of the 25 schools which offer four or more alternative courses, 6 are secondary, 1 is a comprehensive, 9 are community schools and 9 vocational schools. Almost all of these schools work in conjunction with the CDVEC Curriculum Development Unit in

Trinity College, Dublin or with the Curriculum Development Centre in Shannon.

SUMMARY

Three ways of developing curricula have been identified — the central development model, the school-based model and formal pilot curriculum development model.

Pre-employment courses are provided in some 45% of schools eligible to offer these courses. Principals of a further 67% of schools which at present do not provide these courses expressed a wish to offer them in the future.

Of the new Leaving Certificate courses, accountancy and business organisation are provided by over 80% of schools, whereas economic history, agricultural economics and mechanics were availed of least by schools.

In both the case of pre-employment courses and the new Leaving Certificate courses, the size of school appears to be a very important factor in determining a school's ability to provide and to sustain a new course. In the case of the new Leaving Certificate courses, rural schools have made greater provision than urban schools for technical drawing, engineering, workshop theory and practice, building construction, home economics (scientific and social) and agricultural economics.

Forty-four per cent of schools have reported an involvement in some form of school-based curriculum development. The community and comprehensive schools showed very high levels of involvement in this activity. Forty-five per cent of secondary and 33% of vocational principals reported such involvement. Again, large schools are much more likely to offer a school-based course than small schools and urban schools are more likely to offer such a course than rural schools. Pastoral care was the most popular area of school-based curriculum development. Team teaching, health education and enrichment-type junior programmes, including integrated studies, were also mentioned by a significant number of schools.

The transition year and health education projects were the best known of the pilot curriculum development projects, although more than 65% of principals had heard about almost all the projects which had been in existence since the mid 1970's. Since they are still considered experimental and the number of schools is restricted, the percentage of schools involved as pilot schools is relatively small. Some 15-17% of schools have used materials or project ideas, have been, or currently are, pilot schools of the more established single subject projects, whereas 10% of schools have been or are pilot schools of the three interdisciplinary projects. The number of schools which have used ideas from these interdisciplinary projects is much larger.

Sixty-two per cent of schools which responded to the survey are involved in pre-employment courses, school-based curriculum or a pilot curriculum development project. Almost every comprehensive and community school reported this involvement as did more than 75% of vocational schools and 50% of secondary schools. Eighteen per cent of these schools are involved in two such projects and 7% are involved in three or more of the alternative courses. Of the twenty-five schools which reported the greatest amount of involvement with curriculum development projects, six were secondary, one comprehensive, nine community and nine vocational schools. Almost all these schools work with either the CDVEC Curriculum Development Unit or the Curriculum Development Centre in Shannon.

4.

SUPPORTS AND CONSTRAINTS

Principals were asked to rate different variables which could reasonably be counted as either significant teacher supports or general constraints. The items chosen were derived from a general review of the literature[1], from interviews with school principals, and document analysis.

In each case the percentage response to each variable to each of the seven points on the scale was worked out. By comparing the percentage responses at the various points on the scale it is possible to suggest which items are considered most important.

In case any important source of support or constraint was omitted, an open-ended question was placed after the list in which principals could add other items they considered important. In the section on support a further question was asked about what things should be done to benefit teachers with regard to inservice training. In the section on constraints, in addition to the open-ended question asking for other constraints, there was a final question asking principals to rank the three most important constraints.

TEACHER SUPPORTS

We identified nine:
Support from the principal
Short inservice courses
Teacher release to study at a third level institution
Staff department meetings on curriculum matters
Regular meetings with teachers from other schools
Curriculum materials/packages from external sources
Regular release from teaching to plan the curriculum (one or two periods per week for planning meetings)
Educational journals/magazines and other printed matter
Advice of inspectorate.

Principals were asked to rate each of them on a seven-point scale ranging from: very important to very important (Table 4.1). Most of them regarded all nine sources of support as important.

Table 4.1

PERCENTAGE OF PRINCIPALS RATING SOURCES OF TEACHER SUPPORT ON A SEVEN-POINT SCALE

	UNIMPORTANT				IMPORTANT		
	Very	Quite	Slightly	Equally	Slightly	Quite	Very
	%	%	%	%	%	%	%
Support from principal	0.6	0.4	0.0	1.2	2.2	15.8	79.8
Short inservice courses	0.4	0.6	0.6	1.9	4.0	30.1	62.5
Teacher release to study at third level institution	3.3	3.2	7.4	11.9	20.3	34.6	19.3
Staff/department meetings on curriculum matters in school	0.2	0.2	1.0	2.8	7.5	30.2	58.1
Regular meetings with teachers from other schools	0.8	1.2	3.8	10.7	20.1	47.7	15.7
Curriculum materials/packages from external sources	1.2	1.5	3.2	11.8	18.5	40.9	23.0
Regular release from teaching to plan the curriculum (one or two periods per week: planning meetings)	4.2	4.5	5.2	8.0	18.2	29.8	30.0
Educational journals/magazines and other printed matter	0.6	1.2	4.4	10.3	20.4	38.6	24.5
Advice of inspectorate	2.3	0.4	1.4	5.9	10.5	34.5	45.0

These sources of support were then investigated further to find out which were considered the most important. Table 4.2 shows the rank order of these sources of support.

When the sources of support were analysed by type of school, there were no significant differences between principals' attitudes on 8 of the 9 sources. Regular inter-school teacher meetings were viewed as more important in vocational and community schools than in secondary and comprehensive schools.

Table 4.2

RANKING OF SOURCES OF TEACHER SUPPORT
(1-9 Most Important to least)

Source of Support	Rank
Principal	1
Short inservice courses	2
Staff departmental meetings	3
Advice of inspectorate	4
Educational journals	5
Curriculum materials from external sources	6
Teacher release for curriculum planning	7
Inter-school meetings	8
Teacher release to study at third level institutions	9

The ranking above is derived from the consideration of the median score in Table 4.1.

It is not surprising that principals consider themselves important: they control resources and (subject to management committees in schools where they exist) have the power of decision making in most matters relating to curriculum provision. However, it was as a means of support that they rated themselves so important, and the notion of support implies co-operation with others and, in this case, normally classroom teachers. Support in terms of resources, time-tabling allocation, staff deployment, out of school activities, etc, as well as support in terms of ideas and fostering creativity among staff is part of the role of the principal.

Short inservice courses were rated very highly by principals. The courses run by the Irish Association for Curriculum Development, which last for one-and-a-half teaching days, and normally take the form of a workshop or lecture followed by discussion, are typical short inservice courses. Replies to the next question showed principals favour local courses. They also recognise the need for short practical courses rather than longer and more theoretical courses such as one normally takes while studying at third level institutions. Their purpose is to impart ideas and skills on specific curriculum matters and to support teachers as they become involved in different curriculum projects.

Staff meetings on curriculum matters were also rated very highly by principals. This recognises two very important aspects of curriculum development. A primary focus for development should be the analysis of the needs of the students. This is a matter for the staff to work out at meetings. Secondly the process of curriculum development demands consultation between principal and staff and between members of staff.

Thus the three sources of support listed as most important by principals are the principals' own role both in leading and supporting, staff and departmental meetings, inservice courses to develop new skills and to spread ideas.

Each of the three factors ranked next — advice from inspectors, educational journals and curriculum materials from other sources — relate to support from outside the schools.

One of the factors involved people — inspectors — and the other two factors involved things — curriculum materials and educational journals.

The remaining three factors — teacher release for curriculum planning meetings, regular inter-school and teacher meetings and teacher release for study at third level institutions are considered the least important sources of support.

Principals appreciate the long-term benefits of regular release of staff from teaching either to plan the curriculum or to study at third level institutions. However, those long-term benefits must be gained by the loss of teachers to the classroom and principals, faced with the practical demands of the teaching programme, express a preference for those supports that least increase these demands. Thus, in the later questions about inservice courses, release from school with substitution arrangements was rated highly.

Table 4.3 classifies the responses by size of school. In most cases, size of school does not affect the importance of the factors as viewed by principals. However, some interesting differences do emerge. Ninety-three per cent of principals of large schools rate staff meetings as quite or very important, whereas 84% of principals of small schools do so. Fifty-five per cent of principals of large schools rate meetings of teachers from other schools as quite or very important whereas 66% of principals from small schools do. The same difference in responses between large and small schools is found with regard to the importance of educational journals. Finally, only 49% of principals from small schools consider regular release from teaching for curriculum planning quite or very important, whereas 69% of principals from large schools do so. The reason for these differences in the responses of principals from large and small schools may probably be

Table 4.3

RATING OF SOURCES OF SUPPORT BY SCHOOL SIZE

Sources of Support	Quite/Very Important			Unimportant		
	Small %	Medium %	Large %	Small %	Medium %	Large %
Principal	92.5	96.5	98.6	2.1	0.8	0.0
Short inservice courses	90.4	93.4	94.3	0.7	2.2	1.4
Staff department all meetings	84.0	89.5	93.0	1.4	1.9	0.0
Advice of inspectorate	73.7	84.1	73.3	2.8	4.6	4.2
Educational journals	65.3	64.2	56.3	8.4	5.4	5.6
Curriculum materials from external sources	62.7	67.1	54.9	7.0	6.0	2.8
Teacher release for curriculum planning	49.0	63.6	68.6	18.9	11.8	11.5
Inter-school meetings	65.6	64.5	55.0	6.2	6.0	4.2
Teacher release to study at third level institution	50.7	58.4	46.3	17.1	10.6	18.8

accounted for as follows.

Staff meetings are considered more important in large schools because the informal communication system of a small school becomes less adequate as the number of teachers in a staff grows. However, in a large school the principal is likely to regard external support in terms of meetings with teachers from other schools (and perhaps of journals) as less important than his counterpart in a small school which because of lack of numbers cannot have the same range of skills among its staff. Therefore contact with other schools is more important to the small school. Finally, regular release from teaching is a feature of large schools: they have posts of responsibility and subject-based departments which facilitate this.

If the planning and communication necessary for curriculum development is to take place in a large school some pattern of release is probably necessary. Planning and communication are equally important in the small school but are perhaps easier to accomplish as there will be a smaller number of teachers involved.

The next question in the survey requested principals to list any other factors which they considered supportive of teacher involvement in curriculum development. The 235 replies to this question were analysed, and resulted in the identification of five other factors which had not been mentioned in the survey. They were parents, financial support, having a supportive school structure, an attitude among teachers which was open to change, and a flexibility in approach from the Department of Education.

Finally, principals were asked with regard to inservice education what things should be done to benefit teachers in their school. The 524 replies to this open-ended question were classified under nine categories (Table 4.4). Local inservice courses (42% of the replies) were considered by far the most beneficial. The next most frequently mentioned category (17% of the

Table 4.4

ASPECTS OF INSERVICE EDUCATION MOST BENEFICIAL TO TEACHERS

	Number of Replies	Percentage of Replies
Local inservice courses	218	41.6
Release from school with substitution arrangement	89	17.0
Financial support	58	11.1
Expert help (speakers, etc)	42	8.0
New courses/materials	24	4.6
Inservice courses by an outside agency (e.g., teachers' centre)	21	4.0
The inspectorate	16	3.1
General curriculum information	8	1.5
Other	48	9.1
Total	524	100

replies) was release from school with substitution arrangements. Financial support (11%) and expert help from outside the school (8%) were the other significant categories. New courses or new materials, inservice courses by an outside agency, the inspectorate and general curriculum information were also mentioned.

When these replies were analysed by location to determine whether needs for inservice courses varied between urban and rural areas, no significant differences were found. Local short inservice courses were believed to be the most beneficial by 55% of rural principals and by 47% of urban principals.

CONSTRAINTS

MacDonald and Rudduck[2] have suggested that it is a major responsibility of curriculum developers to take account of the system's constraints. It is unrealistic to seek to bring about change as if the present system did not exist. In the development of a model for school-based curriculum development, Skilbeck[3] argues that all curriculum change agents must first of all conduct a 'situational analysis' which would attempt to clarify and identify the internal and external constraints within the school setting before attempting to identify educational objectives or develop instructional programmes.

Gross, Gacguinta and Bernstein[4], have identified some of the major barriers to successful organisational change in United States schools: teachers are often unclear about proposed innovations; they lack knowledge and skills for implementing curriculum changes; there is often a lack of national resources and materials; and finally, inadequate organisational arrangements within the school militate against new developments.

The purpose of the present study was to collect empirical evidence concerning principals' perceptions and attitudes to certain system constraints, and to measure the relative importance to these.

In pilot research with school principals and curriculum developers, and through a review of relevant literature[5], we identified twelve constraints:

— the examination system
— financial reasons/costs
— lack of inservice training
— lack of commitment of teachers to curriculum development
— lack of time to implement innovations properly
— organisational arrangements/structure of school
— lack of parental support

Table 4.5

PERCENTAGE OF PRINCIPALS RATING CONSTRAINTS ON A SEVEN-POINT SCALE

	UNIMPORTANT				IMPORTANT		
	Very	Quite	Slightly	Equally	Slightly	Quite	Very
	%	%	%	%	%	%	%
The exam system	2.5	1.6	2.2	5.5	10.6	29.5	48.1
Financial reasons/costs	2.8	2.9	3.8	5.1	13.4	32.5	39.5
Lack of inservice education and training	1.0	2.1	2.8	3.9	11.9	38.2	40.1
Lack of commitment of teachers to curriculum development	4.8	4.2	4.9	8.8	17.2	30.6	29.5
Lack of time to implement innovations properly	1.5	1.7	2.1	5.0	8.7	35.9	45.2
Organisational arrangement/structure of school	3.5	3.4	3.0	10.5	17.6	34.8	27.2
Lack of parental support	8.3	6.0	6.7	16.1	19.3	22.4	21.2
Lack of resources/facilities/material	2.1	3.5	4.6	7.2	14.4	30.2	38.0
Rules and programmes for schools	4.8	1.6	4.3	9.2	15.5	30.8	33.8
School management	16.6	8.3	5.3	11.6	12.4	20.5	25.3
Teachers' lack of knowledge or skills	4.0	3.8	3.9	9.3	14.2	31.0	33.8
Teacher-pupil ratio	2.6	2.6	2.4	5.0	10.8	24.0	52.6

—   lack of resources/facilities/materials
—   rules and programmes for schools
—   school management
—   teachers' lack of knowledge or skills
—   teacher/pupil ratio.

Principals were asked to rate these items on the same seven-point scale between very unimportant and very important.

Table 4.5 summarises the number and percentage of replies to each constraint on each point of the scale. Factors which most principals rated as very or quite important were considered major constraints and factors which many did not rate very or quite important and which a significant minority rated as 'unimportant' were considered as minor constraints.

The data in Table 4.6 shows the median rank order of these constraints.

It is reasonable to expect that the major problems facing school principals (and teachers) will be located in the hierarchy of barriers to innovation. At the top of the list are: teacher/pupil ratio, the examination system, lack of time to implement curriculum innovations and lack of inservice education and training. These results strongly suggest that principals believe the internal constraints (teacher/pupil ratio and the necessary time to implement curriculum experiments properly) and the external ones (the examination system and inservice education) are major.

Table 4.6

RANKING OF CONSTRAINTS ON CURRICULUM DEVELOPMENT*

Constraint	Rank
Teacher-pupil ratio	1
The examination system	2
Lack of time to implement innovations	3
Lack of inservice education and training	4
Financial reasons	5
Lack of resources, facilities, materials	6
Rules and programmes for schools	7
Teachers' lack of knowledge or skills	8
Organisational arrangements - school structure	9
Lack of commitment of teachers	10
Lack of support from parents	11
School management	12

*The ranking above is derived from the consideration of the median score in Table 4.5.

Furthermore, it would appear that each of these constraints does not lend itself to in-school solutions, that is, the solution of these problems lies outside the decision making power of principals. Principals can do very little to change the teacher/pupil ratio or to lift the pressures imposed by a public examination system.

Teacher/pupil ratio was considered the most important constraint by principals. The importance attached to this is also reflected in the low priority given to releasing teachers from teaching to plan the curriculum which was considered the third least important source of support (see Table 4.2). Release of teachers for this would normally be included within the ratio and so any large amount of teacher release will mean that classes in the school are slightly larger, or that adequate substitution arrangements are allowed.

The examination system was also rated as a major constraint and this congrues with the 85% of principals who would like to see greater teacher involvement in the assessment of their own pupils in connection with public examinations. The examination system as it is at present constituted also contributes to the lack of time to implement innovation which was considered the third most important constraint.

It is interesting that lack of time to implement innovations was placed near the top of this hierarchy, because it implies that innovation is already taking place. What principals seem to be saying is that, because of other constraints which presumably are the amount of syllabi to be covered for the state examinations, there is not time to implement innovations properly, without increasing the length of the school week.

The need for inservice training particularly through short courses and local courses has been described earlier in this chapter. Ninety-three per cent of principals considered short inservice courses quite or very important sources of support (see Table 4.2) and 524 responses were made to the question what aspects of inservice education were most beneficial to teachers (see Table 4.4).

Financial reasons and lack of resources were the next two constraints listed by principals. Financial support was also listed by 11% of principals in their replies about aspects of inservice education most beneficial to teachers. While it was rated among the middle order of constraints here, financial support was more highly rated when principals were asked to rank the three most important constraints on curriculum development (presumably because financial reasons and lack of facilities are treated together in the later question).

At the bottom of the list were lack of commitment of teachers to curriculum development, lack of parental support, and school management. This suggests that principals have a firm belief in the motivation of their staff as well as the support of parents and school management.

A recent research report[6] into the impact of the Schools' Council on curriculum development in Britain found that the most powerful constraints were: cost, lack of resources, lack of time to implement effectively new innovations, teacher attitudes to curriculum development, and the external examination system in prohibiting the take-up of new curriculum projects. The differences between these two hierarchies show that pupil/teacher ratio and the examination system are considered greater barriers in Ireland, whereas cost and lack of resources are considered more important in the Schools Council study. Lack of time to implement innovations was placed high in both studies.

Principals were then asked to rank the three constraints they considered the most important.

This was an open-ended question and the 1,375 replies were categorised under nine headings. Table 4.7 lists the number and percentage of replies in each category, for the three most important constraints on curriculum development. Thirty of the schools did not respond to this question.

When asked to rate the most important barrier, 34% said the examination system. The significance of this response is emphasised by the fact that the factor rated next was mentioned by only 13% of principals.

Financial reasons, personal commitment of teachers including lack of skills and teacher/pupil ratio were all rated as the most important barriers by more than 10% of the principals. Although financial reasons was only rated first by 12% of principals it was mentioned in the most important three barriers by more than 50% of the principals.

Personal commitment of teachers and lack of skills have been grouped together in this ranking. This may explain its higher rating than on the seven-point scale considered earlier when they were separated. Inservice training is surprisingly low in this ranking considering the importance attached to it in earlier replies. The only explanation that is consistent with other replies is that in the answer principals emphasised 'lack of skills' rather than the potential remedy to the lack of skills through inservice training.

While there are some internal differences between the principals' ratings on the seven-point scale (see Table 4.5 and 4.6) and their ranking in order of importance of the three most important constraints (see Table 4.7), there is general agreement that the examination system, lack of inservice training, teacher/pupil ratio, finance and time are the major constraints.

Finally, there was an open-ended question in which principals were asked to specify any other constraints on curriculum development which

Table 4.7

THE THREE MOST IMPORTANT CONSTRAINTS AS RATED BY PRINCIPALS

	1st		2nd		3rd		% of Schools*
	N	%	N	%	N	%	
The examination system	173	34.3	53	10.5	47	9.3	54.1
Financial reasons	57	11.6	116	23.2	87	17.2	52.0
Personal commitment of teachers including lack of skill	63	12.5	86	17.0	67	13.3	42.8
Teacher-pupil ratio	58	11.3	36	7.1	47	9.3	27.7
Lack of time	32	6.5	36	7.1	60	11.9	25.5
Lack of inservice training	22	4.4	47	9.3	52	10.3	24.0
Rules/programmes of Department	27	5.4	25	5.0	20	4.0	14.4
Lack of parental support	8	1.4	21	4.2	20	4.0	9.6
Other	34	7.0	45	8.9	39	7.7	23.6
No reply	30	5.9	40	7.9	66	13.1	—

*That rate the constraint in the first three.

had not been mentioned. The factors mentioned included parental and pupil pressure for results in examinations, school buildings, lack of credit for innovations, and the centralised nature of the system of education.

When the responses of principals to all the questions about constraints were analysed, there were no significant differences between sizes of school and types of school. Principals throughout the country considered the same constraints as important.

SUMMARY

Nine sources of support were identified and all were considered to be very important. Principals consider their own role in leadership and support, short inservice courses and staff meetings on curriculum matters to be the three most important sources of support. With regard to inservice education, principals considered local inservice courses to be most beneficial to their teachers. Release from school with substitution arrangements was also frequently mentioned.

Twelve constraints were identified and in their replies principals rated the teacher/pupil ratio, the examination system, lack of time to implement curriculum innovations and lack of inservice education and training as the most significant. They were also asked to rank in order the three constraints which they considered the most important. Thirty-four per cent of principals rated the examination system as the most important constraint.

More than 50% of principals mentioned the examination system and financial reasons among the three most important constraints. In general, principals of all types and sizes of schools, in both urban and rural areas considered the examination system, lack of inservice training, the teacher/pupil ratio, lack of finance and the lack of time to implement innovations as the major constraints on curriculum development.

5.

ORGANISATIONAL ARRANGEMENTS

The provision of curriculum in each school depends on a number of organisational arrangements:

— arrangements for pupil transfer from primary to post-primary school
— the age of pupil transfer
— the alignment of the curricula of primary and post-primary schools
— the grouping of pupils in school
— pupil participation in public examinations
— provision of guidance services in schools
— provision of remedial services in schools
— provision of physical education facilities in schools.

ARRANGEMENTS FOR PUPIL TRANSFER FROM PRIMARY TO POST-PRIMARY SCHOOLS

The subject of pupil transfer from primary to post-primary schools has been receiving increasing attention by educational researchers in recent years[1]. In the Republic of Ireland, several recent studies[2] and the *Report of the Pupil Transfer Committee*[3] have sought to illuminate the complexities of this process. However, these studies have been descriptive and have yielded little in the way of empirical data on a national level.

In the present survey, principals were asked if they did, in fact, have arrangements with 'feeder' primary schools concerning the transfer of pupils. If they answered 'yes' they were then asked to describe these arrangements. They were also asked how satisfied they were with the present arrangements for transfer and to give reasons to explain their answer.

Table 5.1 shows the number of schools that have arrangements regarding transfer from primary school. Only 211 of the 490 principals answering this question said they had liaison with primary schools. Fifty-eight per cent of the schools did not have any arrangement with 'feeder' primary schools. The majority of secondary and vocational schools did not have any arrangements, whereas 67% of comprehensive schools and 72% of community schools did.

Table 5.1

ARRANGEMENTS WITH PRIMARY SCHOOLS REGARDING
PUPIL TRANSFER BY SCHOOL TYPE

Do you have arrangements?	Secondary (N = 310) %	Comprehensive (N = 12) %	Community (N = 29) %	Vocational (N = 139) %	All Schools %
Yes	42.6	66.7	72.4	36.0	42.2
No	57.4	33.3	27.6	64.0	57.8

Table 5.2 shows the same data analysed by size and location of school. Only fifteen per cent of small rural schols have arrangements with primary schools as opposed to 35% of medium rural schools and 72% of large rural schools. When urban schools were analysed this trend is repeated. Seventy-four per cent of large schools have formal transfer arrangements, while over 40% of small schools and 54% of medium schools have transfer arrangements. It was found that 74% of rural schools do not have arrangements, whereas 57% or urban schools do.

Table 5.2

PERCENTAGE OF SCHOOLS WITH PUPIL TRANSFER ARRANGEMENTS
BY SIZE AND LOCATION

Rural (N = 236) %				Urban (N = 267) %			
Small	Medium	Large	All Schools	Small	Medium	Large	All Schools
15.0	35.0	72.4	26.3	40.5	53.8	74.4	56.5

Principals of the 211 schools who had replied they had arrangements were then asked to describe these arrangements. The answers to this open-ended question wre coded into nine categories. The 306 replies which came from 209 different schools are given in Table 5.3. Liaison is mainly carried out through contact with the principal and teachers of the primary school and through visits to the primary school. This accounts for 56% of the replies. Transfer of records/reports (13%) and priority given to local schools (10%)

are the next most frequent replies. Open days or induction days, parent consultation, and entrance examinations are the three other main categories of replies but all are relatively infrequent.

Table 5.3

NATURE OF ARRANGEMENTS EXISTING WITH PRIMARY SCHOOLS
CONCERNING PUPIL TRANSFER

	Number of Replies	% of Total
Contact with principal	41	13.4
Contact with teachers and principal	64	20.9
Visit to primary school	66	21.6
Open day at secondary school/induction day	20	6.5
Transfer of records/reports	39	12.7
Priority to local schools	30	9.8
Parent consultation	16	5.2
Entrance examination	17	5.6
Other	13	4.2
Total	306	100.0

The data suggest a variety of arrangements are used, with personal contact and visits the most frequent. However, it must be remembered that the replies came from a minority of schools and that the majority (58%) said they had no arrangements regarding transfer. The *Report of the Pupil Transfer Committee* estimated around 20% of pupils entering post-primary school suffered from serious problems of an emotional, social or intellectual nature. Transfer procedures should ensure the special needs of these pupils are met immediately. At present, liaison is largely limited to contact between principals. Much more contact between classroom teachers in the two levels of education is required. More adequate pupil profiling would also seem to be an advantage. In particular, Doyle has argued that 'it seems essential that there should be personal contact between sixth class Primary School teachers and First Year Post-Primary teachers'.[4]

Principals were then asked to rate on a five-point scale between 'extremely satisfied' and 'very dissatisfied', their answer to the question 'How satisfied were they with the present arrangements for pupil transfer from primary to post-primary school?' Tables 5.4 and 5.5 set out the rates of principals' satisfaction with present transfer arrangements analysed by type and size of school. Nine per cent of principals said they were extremely satisfied and a further 48% said they were fairly satisfied with the present pupil transfer arrangements. Fifteen per cent were uncertain and a further 29% were either fairly or very dissatisfied with the present arrangements. Principals of vocational schools were the least satisfied with 44% of those who responded stating they were dissatisfied as opposed to 23% of secondary school principals. Principals of the community and comprehensive schools appeared the most satisfied with their existing arrangements. This may in part be explained by reference to Table 5.5 which shows that principals of large schools are more likely to be satisfied than principals of small schools. Eighty-one per cent of principals of large schools were extremely or fairly satisfied as opposed to 49% of principals of small schools and 55% of principals of medium schools. Most of the community and comprehensive schools are classified as large and there are many vocational schools, especially in rural areas, which are classified as small. Thus the data may reflect vocational school principals' perceptions of pupils being 'creamed off' for other types of school, or it may reflect the general satisfaction of schools with a large annual intake of primary pupils.

Principals were also asked to state why they were satisfied or dissatisfied with the present arrangements. Replies to this open-ended question were then coded into nine categories, three of which dealt with reasons for dissatisfaction. Of those who were satisfied (38% of the replies), most (29%) said the arrangements were satisfactory, while some (5%) said the appropriate calibre of pupils was coming to their school.

The following are examples of the replies received from those who expressed satisfaction:

— The system works well in most cases.
— Students and parents are gradually introduced into school. The Pastoral Care system caters for students during their early work. We have regular contact with parents, and focus on methodology during the first term.
— There are not many problems with our first year students about the change to secondary education.
— Our junior school feeds into the secondary school.

A variety of reasons were given by the 62% of respondents who were dissatisfied with the existing arrangements. Lack of liaison with the

Table 5.4

PRINCIPALS' ATTITUDES TOWARDS PRESENT PUPIL TRANSFER ARRANGEMENTS BY TYPE OF SCHOOL

	Secondary (N = 306) %	Comprehensive (N = 12) %	Community (N = 31) %	Vocational (N = 139) %	All Schools %
Extremely satisfied	8.8	16.7	25.8	5.8	8.8
Fairly satisfied	51.0	66.7	51.6	38.8	47.7
Uncertain	17.3	6.0	9.7	11.5	15.0
Fairly dissatisfied	17.3	8.3	9.7	23.7	18.7
Very dissatisfied	5.6	8.3	3.2	20.1	9.9

Table 5.5

PRINCIPALS' ATTITUDES TOWARDS PRESENT PUPIL TRANSFER ARRANGEMENTS BY SIZE OF SCHOOL

	Small (N = 139) %	Medium (N = 279) %	Large (N = 71) %	All Schools %
Extremely satisfied	9.2	6.2	18.9	8.8
Fairly satisfied	39.4	48.5	62.1	47.7
Uncertain	14.5	17.7	4.2	15.0
Fairly dissatisfied	21.1	19.2	11.6	18.7
Very dissatisfied	15.9	8.3	3.2	9.9

primary school (12%), dissatisfaction because of curriculum differences (10%) and many other factors often to do with poor ability of pupils (30%) were the main reasons given. Lack of standardised reporting/assessments (6%), organisational differences (3%), and lack of follow through for pupils with special needs (1 %) were other reasons for dissatisfaction mentioned by principals.

The following are typical of the replies received from those who expressed dissatisfaction:

— Students should have basic literacy and numeracy to enable them to undertake a course at second level.
— The age is too young, and there is a variety of attainment in all spheres of the curriculum.
— The arrangements can be improved especially for the less able.
— The fact that we draw from many primary schools in the area makes real liaison very difficult.
— There is no coordination, no common standard for pupils ending primary school and no transfer of information about pupils.
— We have twice as many applicants as we have places.

AGE OF TRANSFER

The age of transfer has been the subject of several investigations conducted in Scotland[5] and in Northern Ireland[6]. This question has not been adequately explored through empirical investigation in the Republic, although the Minister has recently issued a discussion document on the subject.[7]

Principals were asked if the present age of transfer from primary to post-primary schools was right for the majority of their pupils (Table 5.6). Forty-seven per cent of the principals answered that the present age was right, while 40% answered that the present age was not right. Thirteen per cent of the replies stated that the principal was uncertain whether the present age was right or not. Three-quarters of the principals of comprehensive schools said the present age was right, whereas significant numbers of principals of all other types of schools were dissatisfied.

Those principals who had replied that the present age of transfer was not right for the majority of their pupils were then asked at what age did they feel pupils should change from primary to post-primary school (Table 5.7). Of the 192 principals who replied to this question, almost all would like to see the present age of transfer raised. If, however, the replies of those principals who had previously said they were satisfied with the present age of transfer are added, a more complete picture is given of principals' views about transfer (Table 5.8). One per cent of principals would like to see the age of transfer lowered. Fifty-five per cent say the present age of transfer is right for the majority of their pupils. Six per cent say the age of transfer should be between twelve and thirteen years of age. Twenty-nine per cent say it should be at the age of thirteen and 8% say students should be older than thirteen when they transfer. When this data was analysed by size of school, there was no significant difference and when it was analysed by type of school, the principals of comprehensive schools (n = 12) were the only exception to the general pattern.

Table 5.6

PRINCIPALS' VIEWS REGARDING PRESENT AGE FOR PUPIL TRANSFER FROM PRIMARY TO POST-PRIMARY SCHOOLING

Present Age Right	Secondary (N = 318) %	Comprehensive (N = 12) %	Community (N = 32) %	Vocational (N = 140) %	All Schools %
Yes	45.4	75.0	35.5	50.7	47.0
Uncertain	14.4	16.7	16.1	10.0	13.2
No	40.3	8.3	48.4	39.3	39.8

Table 5.7

THE VIEWS OF PRINCIPALS DISSATISFIED WITH THE PRESENT AGE OF TRANSFER ON THE MOST APPROPRIATE AGE FOR TRANSFER

	Secondary (N = 123) %	Comprehensive (N = 1) %	Community (N = 14) %	Vocational (N = 54) %	Total of Dissatisfied %
Age 11	3.3	0.0	0.0	0.0	2.1
11 - 12	0.8	0.0	0.0	0.0	0.5
12	1.6	0.0	—	—	1.0
12 - 13	14.6	0.0	7.1	11.1	13.0
13	68.3	0.0	71.4	57.4	65.1
13 - 14	5.7	100.0	21.4	22.2	12.0
14	5.7	0.0	0.0	9.3	6.2

*Useable responses were received from 192 of 201 possible replies.

Table 5.8

PRINCIPALS' VIEWS ON THE MOST APPROPRIATE AGE OF TRANSFER*

Age	% of Principals
11	1.0
11/12	0.2
12	55.4
12/13	5.9
13	29.3
13/14	5.4
14	2.8

*Excluding undecided.

ALIGNMENT OF PRIMARY AND POST-PRIMARY CURRICULA

Since the new primary school curriculum was introduced in 1972 there has been general agreement in reports that there should be a close alignment of the curricula of primary and post-primary schools. Several of the formal curriculum projects described in chapter 1 and many of the school-based schemes described in chapter 3 aim to achieve this, and we asked principals whether they felt there was a need for closer alignment. Eighty-seven per cent of the principals replied, 'yes' whereas only 3% said, 'no'. (Table 5.9) There were no significant differences between type, size or locality of school.

Table 5.9

THE NEED FOR CLOSER ALIGNMENT OF PRIMARY AND POST-PRIMARY CURRICULA BY TYPE OF SCHOOL

	Secondary (N = 312) %	Comprehensive (N = 12) %	Community (N = 31) %	Vocational (N = 139) %	All Schools %
Yes	86.2	91.7	96.8	85.6	86.6
Uncertain	11.5	8.3	3.2	10.1	10.7
No	2.2	0.0	0.0	4.3	2.7

This was followed by an open-ended question which asked how closer alignment could be achieved. The 430 replies to this question were coded into seven categories (Table 5.10). Thirty-four per cent of the replies said there should be an increase in the amount of contact between teachers at first and second level. Many of the replies suggested the curricula should be revised. Some 13% suggested both primary and secondary curricula should be made more compatible with each other, while a further 30% suggested how this might be done. Of this 30%, slightly less than half considered the primary curriculum and methodology should be brought into alignment with that of secondary schools and slightly more than half suggested the secondary curriculum and methodology should be brought into alignment with that of the primary school. Seven per cent of the replies favoured the introduction of a transition year or induction programme and a further 4% suggested there should be special training in teaching methods for secondary teachers.

Table 5.10

PRINCIPALS' SUGGESTIONS FOR A CLOSER ALIGNMENT

	Number of Replies	% of Total
Increase contact between teachers at first and second level	147	34.2
Align secondary curriculum and methodology to that of primary	68	15.8
Align primary curriculum and methodology to that of secondary	63	14.7
Revise primary and secondary curricula to make more compatible with each other	56	13.0
Other	45	10.5
Introduce a transition year/ induction programme	32	7.4
Provide special training in teaching methods for secondary teachers	19	4.4

The following are typical replies to this question.

There should be closer and ongoing contact between the teachers of

senior classes in primary and core subjects areas in secondary school.
—   There should be closer cooperation between the primary and post-primary branches of the Department of Education.
—   There should be better relationships between the teacher associations and a more united policy from them in regard to education.
—   All post-primary courses should be based on those of the primary curriculum.
—   The secondary curriculum must be completely overhauled.
—   There should be some 'middle school' teachers who would specialise in 10-15 year olds.
—   There should be a more flexible programme in first year post-primary school; this would be facilitated by having fewer teachers involved in first year.
—   There should be greater audio-visual content and extra emphasis on project work in post-primary schools.
—   There should be greater flexibility in the post-primary examination structures.
—   Having studied the ICE Report with a group of primary and post-primary teachers, I feel that there were many good suggestions in it which should be revived.

GROUPING OF PUPILS

One of the factors which influence the curriculum in schools is the method used by the school to assign pupils to classes. According to Kelly this has become, in recent years, an issue of major interest to teachers. He says 'it is an issue that raises many questions of a far-reaching kind, ranging from the optimum organisational arrangements for it within the school to its implications for the system of public examinations and even for society itself'.[8]

There is emerging evidence that conventional patterns of ability grouping do more harm than good. The bulk of the research on ability grouping has been carried out in Britain, Sweden and the United States, and the results of this research have been inconsistent. Three major studies in England showed no differences in the achievement of slow pupils under mixed ability or streamed conditions.[9] An equal number of studies in the same country showed slower students at a relative disadvantage in streamed classes.[10] As the major objective of ability grouping is to provide academic benefits, it is a significant conclusion that it tends to produce no such benefit consistently but tends to be detrimental to slower learners. The mass of evidence shows it helps few learners and lowers the achievement of many. Research in England[11] has also shown that ability grouping damages the self-image of slower pupils in lower streamed classes. One of the consequences of streaming was that it restricted pupils' opportunities for social interaction.[12]

The next series of questions was designed to find out the ways used by principals to group pupils for instruction.[13] First, principals were asked how most pupils were grouped in their school. Three possible answers were specified:

pupils were grouped by ability (streaming)
pupils of different abilities were taught together (mixed ability)
other (the respondent was asked to specify his answer).

Replies in this third category were subsequently coded under banding/setting and streaming and mixed ability together (Table 5.11). The data indicate considerable differences exist in patterns of grouping of pupils among different types of schools.

Table 5.11

PATTERNS OF GROUPING PUPILS BY TYPE OF SCHOOL

Grouping Practice	Secondary (N = 316) %	Comprehensive (N = 12) %	Community (N = 32) %	Vocational (N = 140) %	All Schools %
Streaming	35.1	0.0	18.8	52.1	38.8
Mixed ability	37.7	58.3	3.1	30.7	34.5
Banding/ setting	13.3	33.3	56.3	6.4	13.5
Streaming and mixed ability	13.9	8.3	21.9	10.7	13.2

Among secondary school principals no one pattern of organising pupils emerged. Thirty-five per cent of the principals of secondary schools used streaming and almost 38% used mixed ability grouping. In comprehensive and community schools mixed ability grouping and banding/setting were the most common patterns. More than 52% of vocational schools use streaming as the main method of assigning pupils to classes. This same data was then analysed by size of school (Table 5.12). As would be expected, mixed ability grouping is used in more than 50% of small schools whereas streaming or banding/setting is used in more than 75% of the large schools.

Table 5.12

PATTERNS OF GROUPING PUPILS BY SIZE OF SCHOOL

Grouping Practice	Small (N = 146) %	Medium (N = 284) %	Large (N = 71) %	All Schools %
Streaming	26.4	44.1	44.0	38.8
Mixed ability	54.1	29.0	13.3	34.5
Banding/setting	6.6	12.7	32.7	13.5
Streaming and mixed ability	12.9	14.1	10.0	13.2

Patterns of Grouping Pupils in Perspective

Streaming: Fifty-two per cent of vocational schools report that streaming by ability is their main method of grouping pupils. Streaming is also used by 35% of secondary schools and 19% of community schools. No comprehensive schools report they use streaming as their main method of grouping pupils. Streaming is likely to take place more in large or medium schools than in small schools. Forty-four per cent of large and medium schools report that streaming is used as the main method of grouping students as opposed to 26% of small schools. Streaming is also more likely to take place in urban schools (42%) than in rural schools (33%).

Mixed Ability: Mixed ability grouping is the pattern most favoured in comprehensive schools and is also used by more than 30% of vocational schools and 37% of secondary schools. It is used by only 3% of community schools as the main method of grouping pupils. Mixed ability grouping is much more likely to occur in small schools than in medium or large schools: 54% of small schools as opposed to 13% of large schools report this method of grouping as the one used most. Again, mixed ability grouping is more likely to happen in rural schools as opposed to urban schools: 41% of rural schools use mixed ability grouping as opposed to 29% of urban schools.

Banding/Setting: This method of grouping pupils is used in 56% of community schools and 33% of comprehensive schools. It is less frequently used in secondary (13%) and vocational schools (6%). It is also much more common in large schools (33%) as opposed to small schools (7%) or medium schools (13%).

Streaming and Mixed Ability: A mixture of streaming and mixed ability is used in all types of school. Twenty-two per cent of community schools report they use it compared with 14% of secondary schools, 11% of vocational schools and 8% of comprehensive schools. Compared with the other types of grouping it is used relatively equally between different sizes of school with large schools using it least (10%) and medium schools using it most frequently (14%).

Principals who grouped pupils by streaming were than asked whether this was done at all grade levels (Table 5.11). The number of responses to this question was 324, although only 185 principals had described streaming as their main method of grouping. The majority of principals in secondary, comprehensive and community schools who previously reported they used streaming as their main method of grouping pupils *do not* practise it at all grade levels. Among vocational school principals reporting streaming in their schools, more than two-thirds say it is practised at all grade levels. When the same data was analysed by size of school it was found that irrespective of size about 56% did not use streaming exclusively.

Lastly, those principals who said streaming was not used exclusively were asked to describe their method of assigning pupils to classes. There were 163 replies to this open-ended question which were subsequently categorised under four headings (see Table 5.14). Forty-three per cent of the principals said they introduced streaming after first year of the junior cycle course. Nineteen per cent said they used subject "setting". Thirty-three per cent said they used partial streaming or banding. The remaining 4% used a variety of other means.

Perhaps the most important question relating to grouping pupils for teaching has to do with the *criteria*, or reasons, employed for assigning pupils to various streams within the school.

At least one researcher[14] has demonstrated that within the Northern Ireland junior high schools, the placement of children in particular streams

Table 5.13

STREAMING AT ALL GRADE LEVELS BY TYPE OF SCHOOL*

	Secondary (N = 201) %	Comprehensive (N = 4) %	Community (N = 24) %	Vocational (N = 95) %	All Schools %
Yes	33.8	25.0	37.5	67.4	43.8
No	66.2	75.0	62.5	32.6	56.2

*Excluding schools which do not use streaming.

Table 5.14

<table>
<tr><td></td><td>Secondary
(N = 109)
%</td><td>Comprehensive
(N = 4)
%</td><td>Community
(N = 20)
%</td><td>Vocational
(N = 30)
%</td><td>All
Schools*
%</td></tr>
<tr><td colspan="6" align="center">PRINCIPALS' CURRICULUM ORGANISATION ARRANGEMENTS
IN SCHOOLS
WHERE STREAMING IS NOT PRACTISED AT ALL GRADE LEVELS
(JR CYCLE)</td></tr>
</table>

	Secondary (N = 109) %	Comprehensive (N = 4) %	Community (N = 20) %	Vocational (N = 30) %	All Schools* %
Streaming after first year	46.8	50.0	20.0	40.0	43.2
Subject setting	20.2	25.0	5.0	20.0	18.9
Banding/partial streaming	30.3	25.0	75.0	26.7	33.3
Depends on range of ability at entrance	0.9	0.0	0.0	0.0	0.6
Other	1.8	0.0	0.0	13.3	3.9

*A total of 163 useable responses were received from a possible 183.

is significantly related to their future educational performance, educational mobility and general academic fate. Theoretically, it should be possible for all pupils to move across streams but it has been shown in the Craigavon study that this proved not to be the case.

Interview data obtained in advance of the major inquiry, coupled with a content analysis of principals' replies to earlier questions, yielded the following six criteria on which pupils were allocated to streams:

— general assessment at entrance
— standardised test result, e.g. achievement tests developed by the Educational Research Centre at St Patrick's, Drumcondra, Dublin
— primary teachers' assessments, e.g. pupil record cards
— secondary school assessment
— pupil ability
— public examination results.

Principals were asked what criteria were used to determine pupil allocation to streams in cases where streaming was used. Four hundred and twenty responses were received from 285 schools. These were then coded using the criteria noted above and the number of replies and percentage of schools using that criterion calculated (Table 5.15). The two major criteria used are standardised tests and assessments carried out in the post-primary school. Each was mentioned by more than 40% of the schools responding. Entrance assessments were mentioned by 21% of the schools. All these methods of allocating pupils to streams are internal to the post-primary school and each is more frequently used than primary teachers' reports, which were mentioned by 15% of the schools.

Table 5.15

CRITERIA USED FOR ALLOCATION OF PUPILS TO STREAMS

Criteria	Number of Replies	Percentage of Schools Responding*
Standardised tests	128	44.9
Secondary school assessment	124	43.5
Entrance assessment	61	21.4
Primary teachers' reports	44	15.4
Pupil ability (other)	39	13.7
Examination results	13	4.6
Other	12	4.2

*285 of the 324 schools which use streaming responded. Each school could make two responses to the question, and 420 responses were made.

Finally, principals who grouped their pupils by ability (streaming) were asked why it was practised in their school and 388 replies came from 282 of the 300 schools which use streaming. The replies were categorised under nine criteria and the number of replies under each heading and the percentage of schools giving that criterion is given on Table 5.16. The two most common types of reply were for the general benefit of the pupil (32% of schools) and for the benefit of weak pupils (26% of schools). Seventeen per cent of schools said that it was for the benefit of good pupils. The needs of the syllabus and the beliefs of the teacher were each mentioned by 21% of schools. Parental beliefs, however, were only mentioned by 2% of schools.

PUPIL PARTICIPATION IN PUBLIC EXAMINATIONS

Perhaps no other issue connected with the curriculum has caused so much discussion in recent years as that of public examinations. This part of the

Table 5.16

THE REASONS FOR ALLOCATION OF PUPILS TO STREAMS

Reason	Number of Replies	Percentage of Schools Responding*
General benefit of pupil	91	32.3
Benefit of weak pupil	74	26.2
Needs of syllabus	59	20.9
Teacher beliefs	58	20.6
Benefit of good pupil	47	16.7
School tradition	33	11.7
For examination results	15	5.3
Parental beliefs	6	2.1
Other	5	1.8

*282 of the 330 schools which use streaming responded. Each school could make two responses to the question and 388 responses were made.

survey was designed to find out principals' estimates of the number of pupils who enter schools and who subsequently complete courses leading to public examination at Group Certificate, Intermediate Certificate or Leaving Certificate level. In addition principals were asked three further questions:

— what percentage of pupils never sit public examinations?
— what percentage leave school after completion of the junior cycle?
— what other examinations are taken in each school?

The public examination system has been considered by principals as the greatest constraint on curriculum development. Whatever views principals expressed about the need for change both in terms of content and examinations, almost all schools enter pupils for the present public examinations system and it was considered important to establish the rates of participation at the various examinations. In *Rules and Programmes for Secondary Schools*[15] the purpose of the Intermediate Certificate course is given as that of providing a well-balanced, general education suitable for pupils who leave full-time education at about sixteen years of age or, alternatively, who wish to enter on more advanced courses of study. Whether one agrees with this statement or not it is presumably unsatisfactory if pupils begin a course and then leave school before completing it. Thus it is important to establish the numbers of pupils who begin courses and subsequently either complete or fail to complete them.

It must be emphasised that throughout this section it is the principals' estimates of participation rates which are given in percentage figures. These should only be taken as showing a tendency in one direction or another.

The Group Certificate

Principals were asked what percentage of the pupils who entered their school sat for the Group Certificate examination after two years and after three years (Table 5.17). Nearly half of the schools *do not* enter any pupils for the Group Certificate examination. In those schools that do not enter pupils, there are distinct differences when analysed by type of school. Seventy per cent of the secondary schools do not enter any pupils whereas 65% of vocational schools enter more than half their pupils. Further investigation of the data shows that of those schools that do not enter more than half their pupils for the Group Certificate, the majority are entered after two years, while schools which enter less than half their pupils enter them after three years. Schools may enter pupils for the Group Certificate after two years as a 'trial run' of the Intermediate Certificate after three years. Alternatively, the large numbers of schools which enter less than half their pupils for the Group Certificate after three years may be explained by pupils' reaching the legal school leaving age and failing to complete the examination course. It is certainly unsatisfactory to continue to hold a state examination in its present form which is not taken at all by almost half the schools and which is taken by much less than half the pupils, and in some cases as a 'trial run' for another examination.

The Intermediate Certificate

Principals were asked what percentage of their pupils who entered school sat for the Intermediate Certificate after three years or after four years (Table 5.18). Ninety-eight per cent of schools enter pupils for the Intermediate Certificate examination after three or after four years. Of these schools, 92% enter more than half the pupils, and 46% enter all their pupils. Again there are striking differences when analysed by type of school, with 63% of secondary schools entering all their pupils compared with 16% of vocational schools. Further investigation showed that some 14% of schools reported that no pupils in their school sat for the examination after three years. This number is presumably made up from schools which only

Table 5.17

PERCENTAGE OF PUPILS ENTERED FOR THE GROUP CERTIFICATE
EXAMINATION (AFTER 2 and 3 YEARS COMBINED): BY TYPE OF SCHOOL

	Secondary (N = 291) %	Comprehensive (N = 7) %	Community (N = 30) %	Vocational (N = 141) %	All Schools %
None	70.1	42.9	3.0	2.1	44.8
Under 50%	15.9	42.9	81.8	33.0	25.6
Over 50%	4.8	14.3	12.1	41.8	16.4
All	9.2	0.0	3.0	23.0	13.2

Table 5.18

PERCENTAGE OF PUPILS ENTERED FOR THE INTERMEDIATE
CERTIFICATE (AFTER 3 and 4 YEARS COMBINED): BY TYPE OF SCHOOL

	Secondary (N = 317) %	Comprehensive (N = 11) %	Community (N = 31) %	Vocational (N = 141) %	All Schools %
None	1.3	9.1	—	2.1	1.6
Under 50%	1.0	—	6.3	19.2	6.5
Over 50%	34.8	72.7	87.5	63.2	46.1
All	62.9	18.2	6.3	15.5	45.8

offer a four-year cycle to Intermediate Certificate, and the very small
number of schools in which no pupils take the Intermediate Certificate. The
9.1% of comprehensive schools in which no pupils took the Intermediate
Certificate is accounted for by one of the 11 comprehensive schools
responding to this question in the survey. In this school no pupils are
entered for the Intermediate Certificate as a matter of school policy.

School Leavers after Junior Cycle
Principals were also asked to estimate the approximate percentage of pupils
who never sat for a public examination (Table 5.19). Thirty-six per cent of
principals estimated all their pupils sat for some kind of public examination

and a further 26% said all but 2% sat for a public examination. The remaining 38% of principals estimated more than 2% of their pupil intake never sat for any public examination. Ten per cent of principals estimated that 11% or more of their pupils never sat for a public examination.

Secondary schools have the highest participation rate in public examinations, with 78% of schools reporting that at least 98% of pupils sit for a public examination. However, more than 30% of principals from comprehensive, community and vocational schools estimated more than 6% of their pupil intake never sat for a public examination. If one assumes that courses lead to public examinations and that the award of a certificate to the student through the public examination testifies to the completion of a course, then the principals' estimates of the number of pupils who never sit for any public examination is very disturbing. These pupils leave school without completing a recognised course and without any form of certificate.

Table 5.19

PRINCIPALS' ESTIMATES OF PERCENTAGE OF PUPILS WHO SIT ANY
PUBLIC EXAMINATION BY SCHOOL TYPE

	Secondary (N = 293) %	Comprehensive (N = 11) %	Community (N = 29) %	Vocational (N = 135) %	All Schools %
All Pupils	50.5	9.1	27.6	8.1	35.9
98% or 99%	27.6	18.2	24.1	24.4	26.3
95 - 97%	11.6	36.4	13.8	29.6	17.5
90 - 94%	6.5	9.1	20.7	17.8	10.7
75 - 89%	3.1	18.2	13.8	17.0	8.1
50 - 74%	0.6	9.1	—	3.0	1.5
Less than 50%	—	—	—	—	—

Principals also indicated the percentage of pupils who left after the completion of the junior cycle course (Table 5.20). Only 2% of principals of secondary and comprehensive schools estimated that 40% or more of their pupils left after junior cycle, whereas 21% of principals of community schools and 46% of principals of vocational schools estimated that more than half their pupils left after the completion of junior cycle. Sixty-three per cent of principals of secondary schools estimated 5% or less pupils left after junior cycle as compared with 6% of principals in vocational schools. While these figures do not account for pupils who leave one school after junior cycle and re-enroll in another school, they go some way towards confirming the perceived occupational and vocational roles of schools in Ireland.

Secondary schools are more likely to retain their pupils after junior cycle for the Leaving Certificate course whereas vocational schools are more likely to have pupils who leave at the end of junior cycle.

Table 5.20

PRINCIPALS' ESTIMATES OF THE PERCENTAGE OF
JUNIOR CYCLE SCHOOL LEAVERS BY SCHOOL TYPE

	Secondary (N = 307) %	Comprehensive (N = 10) %	Community (N = 29) %	Vocational (N = 134) %	All Schools %
None	10.4	0.0	0.0	0.7	7.0
1 - 5%	52.4	30.0	13.8	5.2	36.8
6 - 10%	14.0	10.0	6.9	8.2	12.0
11 - 20%	14.0	30.0	27.6	13.4	14.6
21 - 30%	4.2	30.0	17.2	14.2	8.1
31 - 40%	2.9	0.0	13.8	11.9	6.0
41 - 50%	1.3	0.0	13.8	17.2	6.4
51 - 75%	0.7	0.0	6.9	23.1	7.5
76 - 100%	0.0	0.0	0.0	6.0	1.7

The Leaving Certificate and Other Public Examinations

Principals also estimated the percentage of pupils who entered senior cycle and who sat for the Leaving Certificate after two or after three years (Table 5.21). Ninety-four per cent of the principals estimated more than half of their pupils who entered senior cycle completed the Leaving Certificate after two years or after three years. Again, the number of students who would complete the Leaving Certificate is slightly higher in secondary schools than in vocational schools. Further investigation shows that four per cent of principals of secondary schools estimated all the pupils who entered senior cycle sat for the Leaving Certificate after three years. In all types of schools a quarter of the principals estimated that less than half of their pupils sat for the Leaving Certificate after three years. In most cases these would be students who were repeating the examination.

Table 5.21

PERCENTAGE OF PUPILS ENTERED FOR THE LEAVING CERTIFICATE EXAMINATION (AFTER 2 and 3 YEARS COMBINED): BY TYPE OF SCHOOL

	Secondary (N = 318) %	Comprehensive (N = 11) %	Community (N = 28) %	Vocational (N = 136) %	All Schools %
None	—	—	—	3.1	0.8
Under 50%	0.6	—	3.0	14.7	4.8
Over 50%	50.3	83.3	72.7	46.9	51.7
All	49.1	16.7	24.2	35.3	42.6

Finally, principals were asked what other public examinations (in addition to the Group, Intermediate and Leaving Certificate) were available to the students in their schools. In all there were 392 replies to this question (Table 5.22). Secretarial examinations were the most frequently mentioned by schools. Fifty-six of the 106 schools which mentioned this type of extra examination were vocational schools. Matriculation was the second most commonly mentioned examination. Sixty-one of the 66 schools which reported students taking matriculation examinations were secondary schools.

GCE was mentioned 39 times, the civil service 31 times, trade examinations 25 times, the Royal Society of Arts 21 times, London City and Guilds 16 times and there were 46 references to other kinds of examination. In secondary schools matriculation, the civil service, secretarial and GCE were the most frequently mentioned. Of the 343 alternative type examinations mentioned only 10 were mentioned by comprehensive schools and 36 by community schools.

PROVISION FOR GUIDANCE AND COUNSELLING SERVICES

There has been in an increasing interest in the provision of special services such as career guidance in recent years. In fact, specialist courses at post-graduate level are now offered by the National University of Ireland at

Table 5.22

ALTERNATIVE EXAMINATIONS AVAILABLE TO STUDENTS
BY SCHOOL TYPE*

Type of Examination	Secondary (N = 176)	Comprehensive (N = 8)	Community (N = 22)	Vocational (N = 93)	All Schools
Matriculation	61	1	2	2	66
Civil service	28	0	2	1	31
Secretarial	35	3	12	56	106
Royal Society of Arts	4	1	2	14	21
Trade examinations	0	1	5	19	25
London City and Guilds	1	1	5	9	16
GCE	21	0	4	14	39
None	39	1	2	7	49
Other	35	2	2	0	39

*392 replies from 299 schools.

Dublin. To find out more about the provision of guidance services in the schools, principals were asked the following questions:

— Does your school have a whole-time guidance teacher?
— Does your school have a part-time guidance teacher?
— If not, do you need a guidance teacher?
— How satisfied are you with the present provision for guidance?

Seventy-two per cent of the principals replied to the first question (Table 5.23) that there was a whole-time guidance teacher in their school. There is, however, considerable variation in provision when analysed by type of school. Only one of the 42 comprehensive and community schools reported that it did *not* have a whole-time guidance specialist. Among secondary schools 78% reported provision for a whole-time guidance teacher while only 52% of vocational schools indicated such provision.

Table 5.23

PROVISION OF GUIDANCE TEACHERS (WHOLE-TIME) BY SCHOOL TYPE

	Secondary (N = 295) %	Comprehensive (N = 11) %	Community (N = 31) %	Vocational (N = 115) %	All Schools %
Yes	78.0	100.0	96.8	52.2	72.3
No	22.0	0.0	3.2	47.8	27.7

When the provision of guidance services is analysed by location we find that 87% of principals in urban schools as opposed to 54% of principals in rural schools say they have a guidance teacher. Only 16% of small rural schools have a whole-time guidance teacher as compared with 24% of small urban schools.

Finally, as one would expect, when analysed by size there are vast differences in the provision of guidance services. Ninety-eight per cent of large schools, 88% of medium schools but only 18% of small schools possess this service. This situation is likely to have deteriorated with a Ministerial decision in late 1982 that schools with an enrolment of less than 250 (what have been termed small schools in this survey) cannot continue to employ a guidance teacher ex quota.

Some schools possess more than one guidance teacher or use part-time guidance teachers in addition to or instead of a whole-time teacher. In their replies the principals said there were 19 schools which possessed more than one whole-time guidance teacher. Sixteen of these were located in large schools, two in medium schools and one in a small school. There were 223 replies to the question about part-time guidance teachers (Table 5.24). Thirty-seven per cent of the schools which replied possess part-time guidance teachers. These part-time guidance teachers either have a certain amount of time allocated to other subjects in addition to guidance or are shared by agreement between two small schools.

Four hundred of the 505 schools stated they had either a whole-time or part-time guidance teacher. Principals of the 105 schools which did not at present have a guidance teacher were asked whether they needed one (Table 5.25). Ninety-six of the 105 relevant schools replied. Ninety-one per cent of these principals replied they did. When these replies were further analysed the principals who did not possess guidance services and who felt the greatest need for them were located in small schools.

Finally, the principals were asked to locate their attitude to guidance provision on a five-point scale between extremely satisfied and extremely

Table 5.24

PROVISION OF PART-TIME GUIDANCE TEACHER BY SCHOOL TYPE

	Secondary (N = 120) %	Comprehensive (N = 6) %	Community (N = 8) %	Vocational (N = 89) %	All Schools* %
Yes	42.5	33.3	25.0	31.4	37.2
No	57.2	66.7	75.0	68.6	62.8

*There were 282 non-respondents to this question: many of these would have no part-time guidance teacher.

Table 5.25

NEED FOR GUIDANCE TEACHER BY SCHOOL TYPE

	Secondary (N = 44) %	Comprehensive (N = 1) %	Community (N = 1) %	Vocational (N = 50) %	All Schools* %
Yes	84.0	100.0	100.0	96.0	90.6
No	16.0	—	—	4.0	8.4

*This refers to schools without either a whole-time or part-time guidance teacher: 96 of a possible 105 principals responded.

dissatisfied (Table 5.26). Sixty-two per cent of the principals expressed themselves either extremely satisfied or satisfied with the provision of guidance services at present. As one would expect from the previous data the schools least satisfied with the present provision are the small schools with 43% answering they are extremely dissatisfied whereas 76% of medium schools and 58% of large schools expressed themselves as satisfied or extremely satisfied with the provision. Vocational schools are also more likely to be dissatisfied than other types of schools. Thirty-one per cent of vocational schools — almost twice as large a percentage as any other type of school — expressed themselves as extremely dissatisfied.

Provision for Remedial Education
There is an increasing demand for wider provision of remedial education in Ireland. In a national survey of reading standards among first-year post-primary schools[16] in 1971/72, it was found that the incidence of backwardness in reading was 16% for the age cohort. In secondary schools it was

Table 5.26

PRINCIPALS' ATTITUDES TO GUIDANCE PROVISION BY SCHOOL TYPE AND SIZE

	Secondary (N = 309) %			Comprehensive (N = 12) %			Community (N = 30) %			Vocational (N = 137) %			All Schools* %
	Small	Medium	Large	Small	Medium	Large	Small	Medium	Large	Small	Medium	Large	
Extremely satisfied	12.9	31.0	16.7	—	42.9	—	33.3	40.0	17.6	7.2	32.7	30.8	23.7
Satisfied	27.1	44.8	38.9	—	57.1	50.0	33.3	40.0	29.4	27.5	38.2	53.8	38.3
Uncertain	10.0	4.9	13.9	—	—	25.0	—	10.0	51.9	8.7	5.5	—	7.0
Fairly dissatisfied	11.4	12.3	16.7	—	—	—	—	10.0	29.4	10.0	5.5	7.7	11.4
Extremely dissatisfied	38.9	6.9	13.9	100.0	—	25.0	33.3	—	17.6	46.4	18.2	7.7	19.7

*There were 488 respondents out of a possible 505.

found that 8.5% of readers were backward whereas in vocational schools the figure was 30% of pupils. Taking the population of backward readers as the focus, Swan found 35% attended secondary schools (which enrolled about two-thirds of all post-primary pupils) while 64% of backward readers attended vocational schools.

In this survey principals were asked four questions about remedial education:

— Does your school have a whole-time remedial teacher?
— Does your school have a part-time remedial teacher?
— If not, does your school need a remedial teacher?
— How satisfied are you with the present provision for remedial education?

Table 5.27 contains the data for the first of these questions. Principals replied that there were whole-time remedial teachers in 36% of schools. When the provision of remedial teachers was further analysed by type of school it was found that comprehensive and community schools were those most likely to be provided with remedial teachers. Only 49% of vocational schools and 26% of secondary schools had remedial teachers.

Table 5.27

PROVISION OF WHOLE-TIME REMEDIAL TEACHERS BY SCHOOL TYPE

	Secondary (N = 273) %	Comprehensive (N = 10) %	Community (N = 29) %	Vocational (N = 124) %	All Schools %
Yes	26.4	60.0	69.0	49.2	35.6
No	73.6	40.0	31.0	50.8	64.4

When the data were analysed by size and location of school (Table 5.28) it was found there were only full-time remedial teachers in 24% of rural schools and in 47% of urban schools. The difference in provision of remedial teachers is even greater when analysed by size of school. Eighty-five per cent of large schools, 37% of medium schools and 10% of small schools possess a remedial teacher.

The provision of part-time remedial teachers was next examined (Table 5.29). There was 291 respondents to this question. Twenty-eight per cent replied they had a part-time remedial teacher and 72% replied they had not. Two hundred and thirty-two of the 505 schools stated that they had either a whole-time or part-time remedial teacher.

Table 5.28

PROVISION OF WHOLE-TIME REMEDIAL TEACHERS BY SCHOOL SIZE AND LOCATION

Rural (N = 212) %		Urban (N = 225) %		All Schools
Small (N = 95)	8.4	Small (N = 29)	17.2	10.3
Medium (N = 110)	32.7	Medium (N = 139)	40.3	37.2
Large (N = 7)	100.0	Large (N = 57)	82.5	84.7
All Rural	23.6	All Urban	47.2	35.6

Table 5.29

PROVISION OF PART-TIME REMEDIAL TEACHERS BY SCHOOL TYPE

	Secondary (N = 196) %	Comprehensive (N = 10) %	Community (N = 11) %	Vocational (N = 74) %	All Scools %
Yes	25.0	70.0	45.5	28.4	27.6
No	75.0	30.0	54.5	71.6	72.4

*There were 214 non-respondents to this question. Many of these would have no part-time remedial teacher.

Thirdly, principals who did not possess a remedial teacher on staff were asked if there was a need for one (Table 5.30). There was 250 responses out of a possible 273. An overwhelming majority (82%) of principals said there was a need for a remedial teacher in their school. When these replies were analysed by size of school it was found that size was not a significant variable in the need for the provision of a remedial teacher. In other words, principals of all sizes of school felt an equal need for the provision of remedial education. When analysed by type of school 89% of vocational school principals expressed this need as did 80% of principals of secondary schools.

Principals were asked how satisfied they were with the present provision for remedial education. As in the case of guidance services they were asked to rate their satisfaction with the provision on a five-point scale between extremely satisfied and extremely dissatisfied (Table 5.31). Sixty-

Table 5.30

THE NEED FOR REMEDIAL TEACHERS BY SCHOOL TYPE

	Secondary (N = 185) %	Comprehensive (N = 1) %	Community (N = 6) %	Vocational (N = 56) %	All Schools* %
Yes	79.9	100.0	85.7	89.3	81.6
No	21.1	—	14.3	10.7	18.4

*There were 250 responses from a possible 273.

one per cent of principals said they were either fairly or extremely dissatisfied with the present provision whereas 31% said they were satisfied or extremely satisfied. When the principals' replies were analysed by type of school significant differences in attitude were found towards satisfaction with the present remedial education provision. The most dissatisfied respondents were principals of secondary and vocational schools. This would appear understandable given that less than 49% of the vocational schools and only 26% of secondary schools in the country possess a full-time remedial teacher. When the principals' replies were analysed by size of school, it was the principals of small schools who expressed their dissatisfaction most strongly. Seventy-six per cent of principals of small schools said they were extremely or fairly dissatisfied with the existing provision as compared with 58% of principals of medium schools and 43% of principals of large schools. Almost 50% of the principals of large schools said that they were satisfied or extremely satisfied with existing provision as compared with 32% of principals of medium schools and 18% of principals of small schools.

Provision for Physical Education

Principals were asked to rate their satisfaction with the present provision for physical education on a five-point scale between extremely satisfied and extremely dissatisfied (Table 5.32). Fifty-four per cent of the principals replied they were either extremely satisfied or satisfied with the existing provision and 38% replied they were fairly dissatisfied or extremely dissatisfied. When analysed by type of school the principals of vocational schools were by far the most dissatisfied with the existing provision. Thirty-nine per cent said they were extremely dissatisfied. When the same data was analysed by size of school the most satisfied principals were those of large schools and the least satisfied were those in small schools. Sixty-five per cent of principals of large schools were satisfied or extremely satisfied as opposed to 60% of principals of medium schools and 38% of principals of small

Table 5.31

PRINCIPALS' ATTITUDES TO REMEDIAL PROVISION BY SCHOOL TYPE AND SIZE

	Secondary (N = 293) %			Comprehensive (N = 12) %			Community (N = 29) %			Vocational (N = 133) %			All Schools* %
	Small	Medium	Large	Small	Medium	Large	Small	Medium	Large	Small	Medium	Large	
Extremely satisfied	4.8	3.6	5.9	—	—	—	—	20.0	18.7	4.6	16.1	16.7	6.5
Satisfied	12.9	20.8	47.0	33.3	42.9	50.0	66.7	30.0	37.5	12.3	39.3	25.0	24.0
Uncertain	9.7	8.6	8.8	33.3	—	—	—	10.0	—	3.1	12.5	8.3	8.2
Fairly dissatisfied	29.0	27.8	14.7	—	57.1	50.0	33.3	20.0	25.0	18.5	21.4	33.3	22.9
Extremely dissatisfied	43.5	44.2	23.5	33.3	—	—	—	20.0	18.7	61.5	10.7	16.7	38.3

*There were 467 respondents of a possible 505.

Table 5.32

PRINCIPALS' ATTITUDES TO PHYSICAL EDUCATION PROVISION BY SCHOOL TYPE AND SIZE

	Secondary (N = 300) %			Comprehensive (N = 11) %			Community (N = 27) %			Vocational (N = 131) %			All Schools* %
	Small	Medium	Large	Small	Medium	Large	Small	Medium	Large	Small	Medium	Large	
Extremely satisfied	20.6	22.8	20.0	—	14.2	—	16.7	31.2	40.0	6.0	18.9	27.3	19.4
Satisfied	27.9	39.1	42.8	—	28.5	50.0	50.0	37.5	60.0	19.4	34.0	27.3	34.2
Uncertain	17.6	5.1	2.9	—	28.5	50.0	—	12.5	—	6.0	9.4	—	7.8
Fairly dissatisfied	8.8	14.2	17.1	—	28.5	—	—	6.3	—	16.4	13.2	18.2	13.6
Extremely dissatisfied	25.0	18.8	17.1	—	—	—	33.3	12.5	—	52.2	24.5	27.3	24.0

*There were 469 respondents of a possible 505.

schools. At the other end of the scale 38% of principals of small schools were extremely dissatisfied as opposed to 20% of principals of medium schools and 17% of principals of large schools.

SUMMARY

Transfer arrangements with primary schools only exist in 42% of schools, and the most frequently used forms of liaison are personal contact and visits to the primary school. A majority of principals said they were satisfied with the existing arrangements for transfer.

Fifty-five per cent of principals considered the present age of transfer was correct, while almost all who were dissatisfied said the age of transfer should be raised.

Eighty-seven per cent of the principals said there was need for a closer alignment of curricula between primary and post-primary schools. Principals were also asked about the methods used in their schools for grouping pupils in classes. Thirty-five per cent of principals of secondary schools used streaming and almost 38% used mixed ability grouping. In comprehensive and community schools mixed ability teaching and banding/setting were the most common patterns, while 52% of vocational schools used streaming as the main method of assigning pupils to classes. Standardised tests and assessments carried out in the secondary school are the most commonly used methods of allocating pupils in schools where streaming is used.

One measure of the success of a course is to establish the number of pupils who begin courses and subsequently either complete or fail to complete them. This may be measured by participation in public examinations. In the survey principals estimated in percentage figures the numbers of pupils who completed or failed to complete various courses leading to public examinations. Almost half the schools did not enter any pupils for the Group Certificate, and in the schools which do enter pupils, a greater number are entered after two years than after three years.

Ninety-eight per cent of schools enter pupils for the Intermediate Certificate Examination, while 92% enter more than half their pupils, 96% enter all their pupils for this examination.

Thirty-six per cent of principals estimated all pupils sat for some kind of public examination and a further 26% estimated all but 2% sat for some kind of public examination. Almost 10% of principals estimated more than 11% of their pupils never sat for any kind of public examination.

Secondary schools are more likely to retain their pupils after junior cycle for the Leaving Certificate course than vocational schools. Ninety-four per cent of the principals said more than half of the pupils who entered senior cycle sat for the examination after two years or after three years and 43% estimated that all their pupils took the examination. Secretarial and matriculation examinations were the most common types of examination apart from the Group, Intermediate and Leaving Certificates.

With regard to provision of guidance services, there were whole-time guidance teachers in 72% of schools. Ninety-one per cent of principals who did not have a guidance teacher expressed the need for one, and 62% of principals said they were either extremely satisfied or satisfied with the present provision of guidance service. These replies were received before the recent cutbacks in guidance provision.

With regard to the provision of remedial teachers, 36% of principals replied there were whole-time remedial teachers in their schools. Eighty-two per cent of principals who did not have a whole-time remedial teacher in the school expressed the need for one. Thirty-one per cent of principals said they were satisfied with the present provision for remedial teachers.

Finally, 54% of principals were satisfied or extremely satisfied with the existing provision for physical education.

6.

FUTURE DIRECTIONS

Principals' attitudes to curriculum development were ascertained. The following three general questions/statements were posed and principals were asked to respond on a five-point scale:

— 'To what extent do you agree that the curriculum of your own school should be the subject of continuous review and development?' The five-point scale ran between 'I strongly agree' and 'I strongly disagree'.

— 'With regard to curriculum change, do you feel that post-primary education in Ireland needs —' The five-point scale ran between 'major changes' and 'no changes'.

— 'Far more changes ought to have been made in the post-primary curriculum in recent years'. The five-point scale ran between 'I strongly agree' and 'I strongly disagree'.

The need to extend curriculum provision was considered. Principals were asked were there any subjects or topics not taught in their school that they would like to see included in the formal curriculum. Were there any subjects taught in their school that they felt had little or no value? In each case, if the response was yes, it was followed by an open-ended question, requesting details of the subjects.

Principals were asked would they like to see greater teacher involvement in the assessment of their pupils in connection with public examinations. If the response was 'yes' it was followed by an open-ended question requesting details of the type of assessment.

There was an open-ended question which asked principals to comment on the types of curriculum changes they would like to see in the future.

ATTITUDES

To the Curriculum as the subject of Continuous Review and Development
Table 6.1 analyses the replies by type of school. There is little difference between the replies: the majority of principals of all types and sizes of

schools in both rural and urban areas strongly agree with the statement. Sixty per cent of the respondents agree strongly and a further 34% agree to some extent. Of the remaining replies none strongly disagreed.

The only difference in the pattern of replies is that 56% of principals of small schools strongly agree, whereas 70% of principals of large schools do. Perhaps the difference may be attributed to the practical difficulty of the process of continuous review and development in small schools. In almost all cases, principals suggest that the image of their school should be one of a self-evaluating institution, carefully monitoring the effects of instruction and innovations and making changes where necessary.

Table 6.1

PRINCIPALS' ATTITUDES TO CURRICULUM DEVELOPMENT AS A CONTINUOUS PROCESS BY TYPE OF SCHOOL

Attitudes	Secondary (N = 314) %	Comprehensive (N = 11) %	Community (N = 32) %	Vocational (N = 140) %	All Schools %
Strongly agree	58.1	54.5	67.7	64.0	60.4
Agree	34.9	36.4	32.3	33.1	34.2
Uncertain	4.1	9.1	0.0	1.4	3.2
Disagree	2.9	0.0	0.0	1.4	2.2
Strongly disagree	0.0	0.0	0.0	0.0	0.0

To the Need for Change in the Curriculum

Table 6.2 analyses the replies by type of school. These data suggest that almost all principals desire changes in the curriculum while a significant minority (30%) desire major changes. There were no significant differences between principals of different types, different sizes or different locations of school.

To the Rate of Change

As with the previous question, more than 90% of all respondents (Table 6.3) agree or strongly agree. Again there are no major differences between size or location of school. There is a difference, however, between type of school: principals of community schools are in stronger agreement with the

Table 6.2

PRINCIPALS' ATTITUDES TO THE NEED FOR CHANGE IN THE
CURRICULUM BY TYPE OF SCHOOL

Category	Secondary (N = 316) %	Comprhensive (N = 12) %	Community (N = 32) %	Vocational (N = 140) %	All Schools %
Major change	30.4	27.3	43.8	28.6	30.4
Some change	68.0	72.7	53.1	69.3	67.8
Uncertain	0.9	0.0	0.0	0.7	1.0
Hardly any change	0.6	0.0	0.0	1.4	0.8
No change	0.0	0.0	0.0	0.0	0.0

statement than their colleagues in comprehensives. Perhaps this reflects the amount of curriculum development already taking place in both these types of schools. More than 50% of the comprehensive schools are already engaged in three or more areas of curriculum development and, therefore, are more likely to agree with the present rate of change.

Table 6.3

PRINCIPALS' RESPONSES TO STATEMENT
'FAR MORE CHANGES OUGHT TO HAVE BEEN MADE IN THE
POST-PRIMARY CURRICULUM IN RECENT YEARS' BY TYPE OF SCHOOL

Responses	Secondary (N = 317) %	Comprehensive (N = 12) %	Community (N = 32) %	Vocational (N = 140) %	All Schools %
Strongly agree	37.1	18.2	53.1	34.5	36.8
Agree	52.7	63.6	43.8	60.4	54.7
Uncertain	5.7	9.1	0.0	0.0	3.8
Disagree	3.5	9.1	3.1	3.6	3.6
Strongly disagree	1.0	0.0	0.0	1.4	1.0

THE NEED TO EXTEND CURRICULUM PROVISION

The vast majority (84%) of principals would like to see the present curriculum provison in their school extended (Table 6.4). There was no significant difference in responses when classified by type or size of school.

Table 6.4

PRINCIPALS' REPLIES TO THE QUESTION
'ARE THERE ANY SUBJECTS NOT INCLUDED IN THE CURRICULUM
THAT SHOULD BE?' BY TYPE OF SCHOOL

	Secondary (N = 300) %	Comprehensive (N = 11) %	Community (N = 27) %	Vocational (N = 132) %	All Schools %
Yes	82.7	72.7	88.9	86.4	83.8
No	17.3	27.3	11.1	13.6	16.2

The 84% of respondents who had replied that there were subjects not taught in their school that they would like to see included, were asked to identify them (Table 6.5). The subjects were subdivided as follows:

— *Arts/Humanities* e.g. History, Geography, Modern Languages, Music, Art, Drama, Irish Studies
— *Natural Science* e.g. Biology, Geology, Chemistry, Physics
— *Commercial* e.g. Book-Keeping, Shorthand, Commerce, Business Studies
— *Technical* e.g. Engineering Practice, Technical Drawing, Building Construction, craft subjects: Pottery, Design
— *Agricultural*
— *Physical Education* e.g. Outdoor Education
— *Social/Personal Type Studies* e.g. Pastoral Care, Social Studies, Health Education, Media Studies, Psychology, Sociology, Civics, Skills for Life courses

Replies classified as appropriate into one or two of these categories, are presented in Table 6.5. The areas of greatest need are those classified under Technical subjects, Social and Personal Type subjects and Arts/Humanities type subjects.

In general the trend is to offer a broader and more comprehensive curriculum. The replies from 30% of secondary schools were classified under Technical subjects and the replies from 34% of vocational schools were classified under Arts/Humanities. In each case it appears principals

Table 6.5

SUBJECT AREAS WHICH PRINCIPALS WISH TO SEE INCLUDED
IN SCHOOL CURRICULUM: BY TYPE OF SCHOOL

Type of Subject	Secondary %	Comprehensive %	Community %	Vocational %	All Schools %
Arts/Humanities	23.0	33.3	21.9	34.0	26.1
Science/Maths	7.5	16.7	15.6	22.0	12.3
Commercial	7.2	—	3.1	2.1	5.3
Social/Personal	27.4	16.7	37.5	20.6	25.7
Technical Subjects	30.2	8.3	15.6	20.6	25.9
Agricultural Subjects	4.1	—	6.2	8.5	5.3
Computer Science	12.9	25.0	18.8	7.8	12.1
Physical Education	1.3	—	—	7.8	3.0
Other	0.9	8.3	6.2	3.5	2.2
Percentage of schools replying	76.1	66.7	78.1	82.3	77.4

wish to offer a wider curriculum by including subjects usually not associated with the type of school.

Twenty-six per cent of all schools replied that a Social/Personal type studies programme should be included in the curriculum. This may also reflect the need to balance the curriculum by adding subjects of this nature, as opposed to what are normally perceived as academic subjects.

The small numbers of schools (5%) which replied that there was a need to include new subjects in the Commercial area may reflect the fact that these subjects are catered for adequately through the existing provision. Accounting and Business Organisation were the new Leaving Certificate subjects with the greatest provision.

Within the Arts/Humanities area, Music, Art and Drama were subjects frequently mentioned by principals.

Computer Science, which is a much more closely defined category than most of the others, was mentioned by 12% of the principals.

Principals were also asked (Table 6.6) if there were subjects taught in their school that they felt had little or no value.

Table 6.6

PRINCIPALS' PERCEPTIONS OF SUBJECTS OF LITTLE/NO VALUE
BY TYPE OF SCHOOL

	Secondary (N = 303) %	Comprehensive (N = 11) %	Community (N = 30) %	Vocational (N = 133) %	All Schools %
Yes	15.2	9.1	10.0	18.0	15.7
No	84.8	90.9	90.0	82.0	84.3

Most of the respondents (84.3%) answered no, while 15.7% answered that there were subjects taught which were of little or no value. There were no significant differences between type or size of school.

As with the previous question, these respondents were then asked to identify the subjects, and their answers were classified using the same headings as the previous question. In all, 93 replies were classified, and the only curriculum area of major dissatisfaction was that of Arts/Humanities and 52 (56%) of the replies were classified under this heading. Sixteen (17%) were classified under the Science/Maths area and 9 (10%) under the areas of Commercial subjects and Social/Personal subjects respectively. The other 7 replies were spread out among the other categories.

TEACHER INVOLVEMENT IN ASSESSMENT

Eighty-five per cent of principals (Table 6.7) were in favour of more teacher involvement in the assessment of their pupils. There was no major difference between replies from different types of school or from different sizes of school. When the replies were analysed by location of school, it was found that 87% of urban and 82% of rural principals agree with the statement.

The 85% of principals who had agreed with this statement were then asked to say what form this teacher involvement would take. Their replies are classified as follows:

— course work assessment including continuous assessment
— project work including field work
— oral examining
— objective-type testing including multiple choice examining

— school-based certificates including pupil profiling
— other forms of assessment

Each principal's reply to the question was classified into one, two or three of the above categories. In all, 683 replies were classified and these are summarised in Table 6.8. By far the most common category is course work assessment. This was mentioned by 71% of schools. Unfortunately, this is also the most general category and could be used as a catch-all. Continuous assessment was also included in this category and was specifically mentioned in many answers. Continuous assessment, assessment of course work, and practicals are the areas in which principals would place greatest emphasis on teacher involvement.

Table 6.7

PRINCIPALS' WISHES TO SEE GREATER TEACHER INVOLVEMENT IN
PUPIL ASSESSMENT IN CONNECTION WITH PUBLIC EXAMINATIONS
BY TYPE OF SCHOOL

	Secondary (N = 313) %	Comprehensive (N = 11) %	Community (N = 30) %	Vocational (N = 139) %	All Schools %
Yes	84.3	72.7	90.0	86.0	84.8
No	15.7	27.3	10.0	14.0	15.2

Many principals gave comprehensive answers to this open-ended question and a sample of their replies is given below.

— Teachers should be allowed to give each student a final examination mark, with this mark given equal weight to that attained by the student in the public examination.
— Continuous assessment of students by their teachers, including home-work, essays, term papers, practical work and projects, to account for at least 25% of the marks.
— I would like to see the continuous assessment of both course work and practical work, as well as attitudes, interest in work, co-operation with others in groups etc.
— A monitored assessment as undertaken with agricultural science, agricultural economics and building construction, if teachers were properly trained and suitably remunerated.
— Continuous assessment of ongoing classwork, oral work and student competencies, with a portfolio of work which is cross-moderated as in the Humanities Project.

— Assessment of course work and of practical work although I know that such staff involvement would mean great disruption to the school, through absence at coordination meetings.

— Continuous assessment should be carried out by the teacher of each subject. A student's final grade should not depend on a 3-hour examination, rather as the result of years of continuous work.

— Continuous assessment of course work, assignment of projects especially in the Environmental Studies area, practical examinations expecially in Science subjects.

— Practical assessment in Home Economics and the implementation of the ICE Report.

— Assessment of course work, practical work and oral examinations resulting in school certification.

— Assessment of effort against ability, assessment of practical work and assessment of faithfulness of completion of set work over a term.

— Assessment of course work. The examination system should veer away from centralisation and tend towards being school-centred.

Table 6.8

INCREASED INVOLVEMENT IN ASSESSMENT BY TYPE OF SCHOOL

Type of Assessment	Secondary %	Comprehensive %	Community %	Vocational %	Total %
Course work including continuous assessment	71.1	33.3	25.0	73.8	71.3
Project work including field work	11.3	8.3	12.5	17.7	13.4
Practicals	32.7	33.3	43.8	33.3	33.3
Orals	10.1	—	9.4	5.7	8.5
Objective type testing	0.9	—	3.1	2.1	1.4
School-based certificates	1.8	—	3.1	1.4	1.8
Other	4.1	—	12.5	5.7	5.0
Percentage of schools replying	80.2	64.2	80.0	84.5	81.2

TYPES OF CHANGES

Four hundred and thirty replies to the question were received and coded into nine categories (Table 6.9) as follows:

— reform of subjects/content
— public examination reform
— a less academic curriculum for weaker pupils
— alternative courses in mathematics
— the reform of teaching methods
— programmes which emphasised personal development
— links with industry/work
— the development of practical subjects
— other changes in the curriculum

As far as the principals are concerned, the two most pressing changes in the curriculum would involve a reassessment of subjects and content and reform of the examination system. Fifty per cent of the replies fell into one or other of these categories. The development of practical subjects, the development of a less academic curriculum for weaker pupils and the

Table 6.9

CHANGES SUGGESTED IN CURRICULA

Type of Change	Number of replies	%
Reform of subjects/content	140	32.5
Public examination reform	82	19.0
Practical subjects developed	48	11.0
Less academic curriculum for weaker pupils	43	10.0
Programmes for personal development	41	9.5
Links with industry/work-place	23	5.0
Reform of teaching methods	18	4.0
Alternative maths course	8	1.5
Other	27	6.5
Total	430	100.0

development of courses which emphasise personal development were all considered as important changes in the post-primary curriculum by principals.

This suggests a curriculum which is less academic and one which stresses the personal, social and vocational development of the pupil. It also suggests that there is need for a major reform of the public examination system in order to assess such a curriculum appropriately. It seems that principals are reacting strongly to the 'bookish' curriculum for everyone, thus identifying the irrelevance of subject-centred curriculum for many pupils.

Many of the principals gave long answers to this question. A sample is given below:

— A new Mathematics course for Leaving Certificate at three different levels to replace the present two courses. I would like to see the higher course staying as it is, the lower course being removed and in its place a course in utilitarian mathematics incorporating a good deal of commercial arithmetic etc. This course should have a standard which would be acceptable to regional colleges and banks etc. A new course should be introduced for students who are good at maths but who are not willing to take the present honours course.

— Such changes as would give us a situation where schools — with proper safeguards to maintain standards — would be free to meet the needs of their pupils without recourse to imposed regimentation.

— More activity-orientated courses for weaker stuents with greater stress on the scientific and practical aspects of education.

— For languages, priority should be given to oral perfection in the particular language with less emphasis on literature and grammar.

— A new form of assessment that will take the emphasis off examining and examination pressure. There should be person-centred work that would inculcate personal initiative and responsibility.

— A module for media education and for education for leisure should be introduced.

— The curriculum should be more pupil-centred than subject-centred with greater emphasis on leisure education as well as responsible attitude formation for constructive use in society.

— Education of a formal nature in secondary schools is too divorced from the employment market and from day-to-day life after school. This should be changed in order to link more to the needs of society.

— There should be greater flexibility to enable schools to cater for local needs. There should also be more scope for self-directed study at various levels.

— More relevant technical education should be provided for students who will leave school at 15.

— A programme should be developed which will counteract the increase in anti-social habits and violence.

— More time and emphasis should be placed on relationships in general personal development so that learning becomes personalised in schools.

— Changes that would make the pupils competent to take up types of employment which would be offered in the future should be available in the schools.

— There should be an alternative course to the Leaving Certificate.

— Courses should be available that would educate the pupils for leisure and unemployment. There should also be courses aimed at developing creativity.

— Counselling and guidance services must be developed in order to cope with the impact of technological development.

— A less academic curriculum should be available to all pupils for five years with a specialised sixth year for those who wish to proceed to higher education.

— There should be greater emphasis on interdisciplinary work and more recognition of practical work in the curriculum.

— Bright students seem to be able to cope with almost any curriculum, academically speaking, but sometimes they lack a general knowledge or fail to see the relevance of what they learn. Weaker students find the academic grind boring and senseless. It is for these students that we must chiefly cater.

—   At least half the marks in examinations should be awarded for oral content in Irish and modern continental languages. There should also be recognition of school-based curriculum.

—   A new general science course for Leaving Certificate students who specialise in humanities or business courses. There should also be a general literature course for those specialising in scientific and other areas.

—   Alternative syllabi less examination-oriented. There should be a movement away from third level entry requirements towards more pupil-centred education which fosters initiative and creativity.

—   A Leaving Certificate that offers a core of subjects practical in nature designed to equip the students for particular types of career.

—   At junior level there should be higher and lower papers in all subjects. At senior level there should be three courses in maths (honours, high pass and lower course level).

SUMMARY

Almost all principals agreed or strongly agreed that the curriculum should be subject to continuous review and development, and that there should be some changes (68%) or major changes (31%) in the curriculum. Ninety-two per cent of principals agreed with the statement that 'far more changes ought to have been made in the post-primary curriculum in recent years'.

Eighty-four per cent of principals said they favoured the extension of the present curriculum provision in their school so as to offer a broader and more comprehensive curriculum. The replies from 30% of secondary schools were classified under Technical Studies and from 34% of vocational schools under Arts/Humanities. Twenty-six per cent of all schools said that a Social/Personal type studies programme should be included in the curriculum.

Principals were also asked if there were subjects offered in their school which they perceived as having little or no value. Of the 16% who replied that there were such subjects, the most frequent response was in the areas of Arts/Humanities.

Eighty-five per cent of principals were in favour of greater teacher involvement with the assessment of their pupils in connection with public examinations. Continuous assessment, course work assessment, and practicals were the areas mentioned most frequently by principals.

Finally, principals were asked to comment on the types of curriculum changes they would like to see in the post-primary curriculum of the future. Of the 430 replies to these questions, 50% stated that the most pressing changes should involve a reassessment of subjects and content and reform of the examination system. The development of practical subjects, the development of a less academic curriculum for weaker pupils and the development of courses which emphasise personal development were all considered important changes.

7.

CONCLUSIONS

Since the data on which this report is based was collected, major educational initiatives have been announced by the Minister for Education, Ms Gemma Hussey. In January 1984 the *Programme for Action in Education 1984-1987* was published and earlier in the same month a Curriculum and Examinations Board was established on an interim basis. In May 1984 applications for participation in new Vocational Preparation courses were invited from schools. Much of the *Programme for Action in Education* directly affects the curriculum. For instance, in the chapter entitled "Second Level Education" it states:

> Major needs will be the reform of curricula and the development of more flexible organisations with particular regard to the needs of the lower achievers and the establishment of a more effective relationship between the education and training system and the world of work.
>
> As an interim measure, pending the outcome of deliberations by the Curriculum and Examinations Board, the Department in consultation with the Board will adopt a flexibility in its rules governing granting schools the necessary authority to introduce alternative curricula . . . The relevant regulations relating to subjects and teaching hours will be examined with a view to providing greater flexibility and encouraging schools to be creative in curriculum change.

The *Programme for Action in Education* also states that action is necessary to assist those pupils who are likely to complete compulsory education or to terminate schooling at the end of the compulsory cycle. Among the measures it suggests is a "better orientation of curricula with back-up remedial and guidance services, stronger links between home and school and increased support for those schools having problems in this respect." With regard to the post-compulsory cycle it suggests that the education and training system must respond to new needs and provide alternatives for those for whom the traditional Leaving Certificate programme is not seen as satisfactory. Health Education, and the place of participative citizenship in the school curriculum are mentioned specifically as is the possibility of expanding existing pre-employment courses and extending them to selected secondary schools.

In the programme there are also several explicit references to the interim Curriculum and Examination Board. In its terms of reference the Board was asked to:

— make recommendations regarding a new unified assessment system for the junior cycle of second level schooling to replace the present Intermediate and Group Certificate examinations

— initiate a review of the Leaving Certificate as a measure of general education and consider how it could be broadened in scope and in the range of skills and qualities measured or whether it should be replaced by an alternative assessment system

— study the desirability and feasibility of introducing a national matriculation examination separate from the Leaving Certificate examination to be used as the principal selection instrument for entry into third level degree courses

— formulate proposals for alternative senior cycle programmes, including programmes geared to preparation for work and those incorporating work experience and/or work simulation.

In May 1984 the Department of Education invited applications from schools which wished to participate in a programme to be known as the Vocational Preparation Programme. This programme will expand existing provision for pre-employment courses and extend them to selected secondary schools, it will adapt existing pre-employment secretarial courses to increase their relevance to changed technological needs in the general employment area, and it will provide one and two year vocational courses for young persons who have completed compulsory education and for whom an academic course is seen to be unsuitable.

In the context of this new interest in curriculum provision, what are the general findings of our survey?

A desire for change
Almost all principals agreed the curriculum should be subject to continuous review and development, that there should be changes in the curriculum and that there should have been ''far more changes in recent years''.

Sixty-seven per cent of principals who did not offer pre-employment courses expressed a wish to do so. Some 15/17% of schools have used materials or project ideas or been pilot schools of the more established single subject formal curriculum projects, whereas 10% of schools have been or are pilot schools of the three inter-disciplinary projects. The number of schools which have used ideas from these inter-disciplinary projects is much larger.

Replies from principals to the open-ended questions about the types of curriculum changes they would like to see in the post-primary curriculum of the future again demonstrate both their willingness and desire for change in the system.

Principals have overwhelmingly expressed a desire and willingness to see change in the provision of curriculum in their schools.

Knowledge and experience of curriculum development
Throughout the survey principals responded to questions about curriculum development in terms of what they are currently doing in their school and not in terms of their aspirations for the future. Pre-employment courses were introduced officially in 1977 and were provided by some 45% of schools eligible to offer these courses in 1982. Forty-four per cent of schools reported an involvement in some form of school-based curriculum development. Although the number of schools involved as pilot schools in formal curriculum development projects is relatively small, more than 65% of principals have heard about almost all the formal projects which have been in existence since the mid-1970's.

Sixty-two per cent of schools which responded to the survey were involved in pre-employment courses, school-based curriculum or formal curriculum development projects. Eighteen per cent of schools were involved in two of the above projects and 7% were involved in three or more of these alternative courses or projects.

The development of the curriculum in some form or other is taking place in a majority of schools in the country.

The direction of change
When principals were asked to comment on the types of curriculum changes they would like to see in the post-primary curriculum of the future they responded in terms of a broader and more comprehensive curriculum. The replies from 30% of secondary schools were classified under Technical studies and from 34% of vocational schools under Arts/Humanities. Twenty-six per cent of all schools said that a Social/Personal type studies programme should be included in the curriculum.

Principals wished to have the content of subjects reassessed and wanted emphasis to be placed on the development of practical subjects, the development of a less academic curriculum for weaker pupils and on personal development.

Sixty-seven per cent of principals wish to offer the pre-employment course. This interest lies in the need to secure vocational skills for pupils at a time of increasing economic recession and unemployment. It may be interpreted as a measure of the success of these courses. It may also be interpreted as a measure of the failure of the present Leaving Certificate to meet the needs of all the pupils who stay in school after junior cycle.

Projects which are initiated by individual schools are also likely to indicate gaps in the current provision at national level which are being remedied by some form of school-based curriculum development. Pastoral care was the most popular area of school-based curriculum development. Team teaching, health education and enrichment type junior cycle programmes including integrated studies were also mentioned by a significant number of schools.

The projects which were considered formal curriculum development projects are also school-based. However, they differ from the previous schemes as they are also funded and derive support from a central or local agency external to the school. The content of many of these programmes such as transition year, health education projects and the inter-disciplinary projects are also likely to indicate the direction of change and content of the future.

1   *Principals favour change towards a broader and more comprehensive curriculum yet one which is more diverse and varied to allow for local needs and ranges of ability.*

2   *Principals favour the development of courses which are less academic in nature, which foster pastoral care and personal development and which emphasise the development of vocational skills. At junior cycle level they are likely to involve some form of integration of subjects. At senior cycle level such courses will emphasise the development of vocational skills.*

Public examinations
Principals consider the present examination system is the greatest constraint on curriculum development. Eighty-five per cent of principals were in favour of greater teacher involvement with the assessment of their pupils in connection with public examinations. Continuous assessment, course work assessment, and practicals were the areas mentioned most frequently by principals for teacher involvement. Several of the formal curriculum projects involved assessment procedures which have been accepted by the Department of Education as the equivalent of Intermediate and Group Certificate for experimental purposes. This involvement in alternative assessment procedures through curriculum development is undoubtedly one of the aspects of the projects which attracted principals.

The Group Certificate is not taken by almost half of the schools which responded to the survey, and of those schools which do enter pupils for this examination many appear to do so at second year level as a "trial run" for the Intermediate Certificate in the following year. The Intermediate Certificate is taken by a very large percentage of pupils from all schools. It is also doubtful whether any examination which is taken at one level (apart from English, Irish and mathematics) can be appropriate to the full range of ability of students who take the examination at present. In answer to another question about the percentage of pupils who do not sit for any public examination some twenty per cent of the principals said six or more than six per cent of the pupils left school without sitting for any public examination.

1   *The present examination system is unsatisfactory:*
—   *some students leave school without ever sitting an examination*
—   *the Group Certificate is not taken by almost half of the schools, the Intermediate Certificate is taken by a wider range of pupils than is appropriate to an examination offered at only one level (apart from English, Irish and mathematics).*
2   *Principals consider the present examination system is the greatest barrier to reform of the curriculum.*
3   *Principals would like to see greater teacher involvement in the assessment of their own pupils.*
4   *Principals consider this involvement should include continuous assessment, assessment of course work and practicals.*

Supports

If curriculum development is to take place it is necessary to know how it should be supported and what are the barriers or constraints that must be overcome. In the survey nine sources of support were identified and all were considered by principals to be very important. Principals considered their own role in leadership and support, short inservice courses and staff meetings on curriculum matters were the three most important sources of support to teachers. With regard to inservice education they considered local inservice courses were the most beneficial to their teachers. Release from schools with substitution arrangements was also considered very important.

The leadership role of the principal, short local inservice courses and staff meetings on curriculum matters are considered the most important sources of support for curriculum development.

Constraints

Twelve constraints were also identified and in their replies principals rated the teacher/pupil ratio, the examination system, lack of time to implement curriculum innovations and lack of inservice education and training as the most signficant ones. They were also asked to rank in order the three constraints they considered the most important. Thirty-four per cent of principals rated the examination system as the most important constraint. More than 50% of schools mentioned the examination system and financial reasons among the most important constraints.

The present examination system, the lack of inservice training, the pupil/teacher ratio, lack of finance and lack of time to implement innovations are the major constraints.

Transfer arrangements with primary schools
Fifty-eight per cent of principals reported they did not have any transfer arrangements with primary schools. Such arrangements are likely to be found more in the community and comprehensive schools than in secondary or vocational schools. Where they do exist, liaison is likely to be through personal contacts or visits. Transfer of records/reports was mentioned only as a type of liaison by 13% of principals. Yet 57% of the principals considered the existing arrangements were fairly satisfactory or extremely satisfactory. Large schools are more likely to be satisifed with their arrangements than small schools. Vocational schools are the least satisfied.

There are no transfer arrangements in a majority of schools, and yet only a signficant minority of schools is dissatisifed with this situation.

Age of transfer
The age of transfer is the subject of much debate and recently the Minister for Education has issued a discussion paper on the subject entitled *The Ages of Learning.* In the survey there was no consensus among participants on this subject.

1   *Principals are almost equally divided on whether the present age of transfer is satisfactory.*
2   *Almost all those who are dissatisfied would like to see the age of transfer raised.*

Alignment of curricula
The vast majority of principals felt there was a need for closer alignment between curricula in primary and post-primary schools. Some felt this should be achieved by more contact between teachers, others that the primary school curriculum should be aligned to the post-primary, and others that the curriculum at post-primary level should be changed to follow on from the primary school curriculum.

There is a need for greater alignment between the primary and post-primary curricula.

Grouping of pupils

Streaming, mixed ability teaching, banding/setting, or streaming combined with mixed ability teaching were identified as the patterns of grouping pupils. No single pattern predominated, and there were also differences between year levels. Streaming is used by 52% of vocational and 35% of secondary schools. Mixed ability grouping is used by most comprehensive schools, and by 31% of vocational schools and 38% of secondary schools. Banding/setting is used by 56% of community schools.

Standardised tests and assessments carried out by the school are the most frequently used criteria for assigning pupils to groups by ability (streaming).

There is no uniform way used by schools to group pupils for teaching purposes.

Provision of guidance and remedial services

At the time of the survey 72% of schools had a full-time guidance teacher and 36% of the schools had a full-time remedial teacher. More than 80% of schools which did not have full-time guidance or remedial teachers desired to have such a provision.

Sixty-two per cent of principals said they were satisfied or extremely satisfied with the provision of guidance services, whereas only 31% of principals were satisfied or extremely satisfied with present remedial provision.

The provision of guidance services in schools is better than the provision of remedial services. The vast majority of principals who do not have guidance or remedial teachers wished to have them.

Size of school

In the survey schools with an enrolment of over six hundred were categorised as large, and schools with an enrolment of less than 250 were categorised as small. The majority of community schools are 'large' and the majority of vocational schools are 'small'. Throughout the survey, principals reported that large schools were able to provide a wider curriculum and were more likely to sustain an innovation than small schools. Large schools are also much more likely to have specialist guidance and remedial services and to be happy with existing transfer arrangements with primary schools.

Large schools are able to provide a wider and more varied curriculum than small schools.

Location
In the survey schools were classified as urban if they were located in a city or town of more than 5,000 and otherwise as rural. The majority of secondary and community schools is located in urban areas, and the majority of vocational schools in rural areas. In general, there appears to be a tendency for urban schools to provide more specialist services than rural schools. Urban schools are more likely to have guidance services, remedial teachers and transfer arrangements with primary schools. They are also more likely to have a school-based curriculum project. Rural schools, however, have greater provision for the teaching of technical drawing, engineering, workshop theory and practice, building construction, home economics (social and scientific) and agricultural economics than urban schools.

In most aspects of curriculum provision rural schools are less well provided.

WHAT ARE THE IMPLICATIONS OF THESE FINDINGS?

1 **The Department of Education and other policy makers**
   Many schools are already taking initiatives to change the curriculum. These initiatives should be encouraged and supported. This can be done by the Department of Education adopting greater flexibility in its rules governing granting schools the necessary authority to introduce alternative curricula. In the *Programme for Action in Education* there is a commitment that this will happen as an interim measure pending the outcome of deliberations by the Curriculum and Examinations Board.
   There is a great need for changes in the examination system. This is a question of central policy partly because of the present centralised nature of the examinations system, and partly because of the need to ensure that in any changes that are made, public confidence in the system and in its standards is maintained. In many subjects there is a need to introduce new procedures which are more flexible and which assess a wider variety of skills. There is also a need to involve teachers in the assessment of their students. It is a matter of policy to establish the rate of change, to establish the types of change and to maintain the standards within the system. The implications of this for inservice education will be discussed below.
   Diversification of curriculum content is necessary if courses which respond to local and community needs and which help pupils with different abilities and special needs are to be developed. In order to encourage this, the Department of Education should produce curriculum guidelines rather than examination syllabi in these new areas.

If curriculum change is to be effective, it is necessary to develop a policy about both the supply and the inservice training of teachers. There is a need for many teachers to develop new skills and knowledge or to update themselves in relation to industry and technology. Vocational preparation and personal and social development were also frequently mentioned in the report as new dimensions within subjects which required greater emphasis. Continuous assessment, project work and practicals are areas of assessment which will demand new skills of the teachers. Inservice education must be established as part of the ongoing professional work of the teacher. This has important resources and staffing implications, but it is vital if changes in the curriculum and examinations system are to become widespread.

It is a matter of urgency that there should be a natural sequence in curriculum and an alignment between the primary and post-primary curriculum. If such alignment existed, at least some of the problems associated with the age of transfer from primary to post-primary school would be overcome.

2   **School principals**

Principals identified their own leadership and support role as the most important support for curriculum development. Traditionally the identification of the school principal with curriculum leadership has been clear. However, recently, many principals consider that the increasing amount of administrative duties they are required to perform does not leave adequate time for this work. Curriculum leadership is not something that can be done in isolation. It demands the cooperation of staff in analysing the existing provision, establishing the needs of students and of the community, setting aims and objectives and translating these into the activities of each classroom. It is in the establishment of this process of review leading to curriculum development that the principal exercises both his leadership and support roles. This must happen if the curriculum in each school is to respond to local and community needs and to help pupils of different abilities and special needs.

The types of changes in content, methodology and assessment procedures suggested in the survey will demand of the school principal a new range of management skills. Implicit in the changes in content and methodology is a wider view of the school as a place from which learning takes place rather than as a number of classrooms in which learning goes on. Field trips, visits to historical sites in the locality, work experience, community service and guest speakers in the school are all more likely to take place. All of these bring with them organisational and administrative problems to be overcome.

Changes in the public examination system to include some element of school based assessment will also affect the school principal. In such a situation the 'examination secretary' is likely to be responsible for the submission of marks in addition to the administration of examination scripts etc on a wider scale than at present.

The consequence of these changes is an increase in the amount of inservice education necessary for teachers. Release of teachers to attend courses and the making of adequate substitution arrangements is already an ongoing problem with which many principals have to cope. If the amount of inservice education increases it will be necessary to allocate to principals greater resources so that they can meet these new demands on their schools.

Lack of information to the parties concerned is one of the problems often encountered in change in curriculum provision. Communication, therefore, is a priority and this has immediate implications for the role of the principal. It is his job to inform the whole staff and not just the teachers concerned in innovation in his own school. It is also up to him to keep the parents and local employers aware of the implications of any change in the curriculum. It is often he who, in the first instance, is the person who represents the school in the community. Thus, he is the central person in initiating dialogue with industry about the establishment of a pre-employment course, with local interest groups about ways of enriching the curriculum through visits, field studies and speakers, or with primary schools about transfer arrangements. While these skills of information giving and communication have always been part of the principal's role, they become even more important when change in the curriculum provision is being undertaken.

3   **Teachers**

Teachers are the medium through which the intended curriculum is turned into what actually happens in each classroom. They are the central agents of curriculum change and without their support, change is not likely to be effective. It is the policy of the IACD that all effective curriculum development involves teachers. The major implication for the teacher is that of a change of role.

For too long, those outside education and even some teachers have held a view of the teacher that restricted his role to teaching in the classroom. This report suggests that the teacher's role should be conceived more widely and that he should be part of each stage of the curriculum process. He should be involved in the planning necessary to establish what should be taught, he should be involved in the evaluation of the success of courses and in the assessment of pupils he teaches.

In addition, the process of curriculum development will mean that teachers no longer work only as individuals, but function as a team, consulting and supporting each other in all aspects of their work.

The need to provide courses which use the local area and which respond to community needs, the need to know more about industry and new technology, the need to teach pupils of differing abilities and to place more emphasis on the vocational, social and personal aspects of teachers all make new demands on the teacher. Inservice education must become a vital component of each teacher's work if these demands are to be met.

4   The wider community

The report recommends that the provision of curriculum in schools should change to enable schools to adapt more quickly to meet the needs of society. Ongoing review, flexibility, greater local responsibility for curriculum and assessment, more inservice education are all frequently mentioned throughout the survey. For the parent, this implies many changes in the traditional concept of the school. It implies that there should be a greater variety and diversity in the curriculum, that the curriculum should be adapted to local needs and specialist interests and that not all the pupils should learn the same things. It also implies that the classroom should no longer be seen as the place within which all learning takes place. Fieldtrips, work experience etc thus become an integral part of each pupil's learning. Finally it implies that the examination system should be widened and that the pupil's teachers should be responsible for allocating some marks within the state examination system.

These then are the implications of the survey for the wider community. Parents and employers must actively wish schools to evolve in this direction if these changes are to become common rather than the exception and if the schools are to meet the challenge of change.

FURTHER RESEARCH

Surveys by their nature raise many further issues which they do not themselves address. Among the most pressing of the issues raised by this survey are:

1. The need for research on the continuity of curriculum experience. Little is known, for example, about continuity from year to year in post-primary education and from sixth class in primary to first year in junior cycle.

2. Research is needed which will focus on the range of experience across the whole curriculum. What concepts, skills etc are being learned at different levels? What is an appropriate ''core'' curriculum?

3. What is the best way of disseminating the experiences which have been gained in curriculum development projects?

4. Studies are needed to examine the machinery of transfer from primary to post-primary school. To what extent have consultative procedures been established between schools? What effect on pupils do different transfer procedures have?

5. There is a need to research appropriate forms of curriculum for the provision of remedial education in terms of materials, teaching methods, pupil activities and forms of assessment.

6. Studies are needed which highlight aspects of conducting school review and evaluation of curriculum, updating teachers' knowledge and skills in using a variety of teaching strategies and experimental materials.

7. Research into the role of teachers as curriculum developers and evaluators is also needed. Such research is likely to involve situation analysis and the employment of action research techniques to evaluate teaching performance.

REFERENCES

Chapter One

1. Department of Education *White Paper on Educational Development*, 1980. Other narrow definitions of the curriculum will be found in E.S. Maccia "Curriculum Theory and Policy", Occasional Paper 65-176, Educational Theory Centre, Ohio State University; G.A. Beauchamp, *Curriculum Theory,* Wilmette, Illinois: Kegg Press, 1961; and Johnston, M. Jr., "Definitions and Models in Curriculum Theory", *Educational Theory,* Volume 17, April, 1967.

2. Johnston, H.T. *Foundations of Curriculum.* Columbus, Ohio, Charles E. Merritt Publishing Co. 1968. Other global definitions of the curriculum will be found in Rugg, H. *American Life and the School Curriculum.* Boston: Ginn and Company, 1936, and W.F. Connell, "A Glossary of Curricular Terms", *The Forum of Education,* Volume 14, 1955.

3. The Open University Course E-283, Unit 1, 1971.

4. Stenhouse, L. *An Introduction to Curriculum Research and Development.* London: Heinemann Educational Books Limited, 1975. The first chapter of Stenhouse's book contains a very useful discussion on definitions of the curriculum.

5. *Compass.* The Journal of the Irish Association for Curriculum Development, is published twice a year by the association, and is available from the Secretary, 1 Bellevue Road, Glenageary, Co. Dublin.

6. Randles, E. *Post-Primary Education in Ireland 1957 to 1970.* Dublin: Veritas Publications, 1975. This book contains a very useful account of developments in Irish education on an annual basis.

7. Coolahan, J. *Irish Education: Its History and Structure.* Dublin: The Institute of Public Administration, 1981.

8. Mulcahy, D.G. *Curriculum and Policy in Irish Post-Primary Education.* Dublin: The Institute of Public Administration, 1981. This book argues for change in curriculum in post-primary schools from a philosohical basis. It is the first of its kind to be published on curriculum policy in Ireland and as such has contributed much to the present interest in the curriculum.

9. Hannon, D. *Sex Differences in Subject Provision and Student Choice in Irish Post-Primary Schools,* Dublin: Economic and Social Research Institute, 1983. This books shows that there are major differences in curriculum provision for boys and girls. It is an area of great importance and one mentioned as a priority in the *Programme for Action in Education 1984-1987.*

10. Coolahan J. *Irish Education History and Structure.* Op. Cit. P.

11. P.J. Hillery's speech on Post-Primary Education (1963) and other important documents from the time are contained in *Reviews of National Policies for Education; Ireland,* Paris: OECD, 1969.

12. Department of Education. *Ár Noastaí Uile — All Our Children* (1969).

13. The two volumes of the *Primary School Curriculum: Teachers's Handbook* were published by Brown and Nolan in 1971, for the Department of Education. In 1975 the Conference of the Convent primary schools in Ireland published an *Evaluation of the new curriculum for primary schools* and in 1976 the INTO Education Committee published *The Primary School Curriculum: Curriculum Questionnaire Analysis*. A very useful summary and bibliography is to be found in "Primary School: whither the curriculum?" by Kevin Hurley. *Compass: Journal of the Irish Association for Curriculum Development* Volume 6, Number 2, (1977).

14. *The Final Report of the Committee on the form and function of the Intermediate Certificate Examination* (the ICE Report) Dublin: Stationery Office, 1975.

15. The City of Dublin VEC's Curriculum Development Unit is managed jointly by the City of Dublin Vocational Education Committee, Trinity College Dublin and the Department of Education. The Unit issues an annual report of its activities.

16. Further information about ISCIP can be obtained from the *Handbook for Science Teachers* 'Dublin: O'Brien Educational, 1982 and the Annual Reports of the Curriculum Development Unit. The student's materials have been published by O'Brien Educational in two volumes 1977, and 1978. For early descriptions of the project see Bridges K., Freestone M., O'Riordan J., Powell B.L. "The Irish Science Innovation Project" in *Compass*, Volume 1 Number 2, 1972, and Trant, A, Crooks, J.A. and Powell B.L. "Curriculum Development in Action" in *Oideas*, Number 9, 1973. The Annual Reports of the Curriculum Development Unit are a further source of information.

17. 13 books for students and 2 teachers handbooks on the Humanities Curriculum have been published by O'Brien Educational since 1976. Aspects of the Humanities Curriculum have been written about frequently, for instance, Godwin N., outlined the First Year Programme and O'Sullivan P., outlined the use of materials on the Aran Islands as a contrast study in *Compass* Volume 3, Number 2, (1974). Crooks T., wrote about "The role of English Literature in the City of Dublin Humanities Curriculum" in the *Proceedings of the 14th Loughborough International Conference on Children's Literature* in Dublin 1981. Several unpublished dissertations for higher degrees contain further information on the Humanities Curriculum. Early references can be found in Crooks T., "Towards a Humanities Programme" *Compass* Volume 1, Number 2, (1972) and in Trant A., Crooks J.A., and Powell B.L., "Curriculum Development in Action" in *Oideas* Number 9, (1973). For a more recent description, see Godwin N. "The City of Dublin Humanities Curriculum: Perspectives of a Decade", in *Compass* Volume 13, Number 1, (1984). The annual reports of the Curriculum Development Unit are a further source of information.

18. 7 booklets on the Social and Environmental Studies Project have been published by School and College Services in 1976 and 1977. See also O'Connor S., *Summary Report of the Evaluation of SESP*. The Curriculum Development Centre Shannon, 1975; and Heywood J., Assessment in History 12-15 Report Number 1. Public Examinations Evaluation Project School of Education, University of Dublin, pp. 1-162, 1974. Further information can be obtained from the Curriculum Development Centre in Shannon.

19. Further information about the Outdoor Education Project can be found in the Annual Reports of the Curriculum Development Unit.

20. The Department of Education published the Proposals as a basis for a Course in Irish Studies (Mimiograph) 1974. MacDonough, P. has described the Irish Studies project in Tallaght Community School in *Compass*, Volume 3, Number 3, 1974. MacMahon M has described the course in Crescent Comprehensive, Dooradoyle, Limerick in *Compass*, Volume 3, Number 2, 1974. For further information about the concept Irish

Studies see Trant A, "The Concept of Irish Studies" in *Compass* Volume 3, Number 2 and Farren S, "Cultural Studies in the Curriculum — A Northern Perspective:" in *Compass,* Volume 3, Number 2, 1974, and for the curricular model in Irish Studies see Callan, J. "Curriculum Development in Irish Studies", in *Oideas,* Number 16, 1976.

21. See *Investment in Education,* 1966, and *Investment in Education — Annexes and Appendices,* 1966. John Coolohan has called the Report "one of the foundation documents of modern Irish education".

22. Manpower Consultative Committee, *Report on Youth Employment,* 1980.

23. Department of Education (Dublin: Stationary Office) *White Paper on Educational Development,* 1980.

24. The Department of Education has published *Guidelines for Pre-Employment Courses* in 1977 and in a revised version in 1978. Further information may be found in *Compass,* Vol 7, No 2, 1978, which contains a series of articles on these courses including two case studies and an initial analysis of work experience. The Department of Education have recently completed a review of these courses.

25. For further information see *Compass,* Vol 11, No 1, 1982, which contains an overview of the transition from school to adult and working life projects and an article by E. Fogarty on Community-Based Learning. Other information may be obtained from the Curriculum Development Centre, Shannon and from the "National Dossier" on the three projects containing the projects' final report, the external evaluation, and the Department of Education's own report. The Commission of the European Communities has also produced a final programme report on the European Community Action Programme, *Pilot Projects on the Transition of Young People from Education to Adult Working Life,* Brussels, 1983.

26. For further information on this project see the above reference for the European context. See also *A Survey of the Attitudes and Expectations of Second Level School-Leavers,* Irish Foundation for Human Development, 1977; and "Education for Development", by L. Kealy in *Compass,* Vol 11, No 1, 1982. Further information on the project can be obtained from the Irish Foundation for Human Development.

27. For further information on this project see reference 25 for the European context. See also "The work of the Early School-Leavers Project" by G. Granville in *Compass,* Vol 11, No. 1, 1982, a series of six reports on different elements of the project and *Educational Achievement and Youth Employment,* the proceedings of the dissemination seminar. Further information can be obtained from the Curriculum Development Unit.

28. IFA Plan *Thirty Pilot Projects. Short Description of the 30 Pilot Projects in the European Community's Second Transition Programme.* Koln 1984.

29. County Tipperary (NR) VEC, *Post-Primary Education 1985-2000 and its Relevance to the Economy* and "An Exercise in School/Scheme-Based Curriculum Development: The Tipperary (NR) VEC Alternative Mathematics Programme" by John O'Donoghue and Luke Murtagh in *Compass,* Vol. 12, No. 1, 1983. See also reference 34 below.

30. See the Annual Reports of the Curriculum Development Unit and *Report on Provision at Senior Cycle Level in CDVEC and Other Schools 1983* by the Curriculum Development Unit, 1984.

31. The Irish Association for Curriculum Development adopted a document *Establishing Priorities in the Curriculum* in 1977 as its policy. The six principles are as follows:
— the curriculum should cater for the needs of all students;
— the curriculum should be responsive to the needs of all society;
— the curriculum should follow a natural sequence;
— examinations should conform to the needs of the curriculum;
— all effective curriculum development involves teachers;

— innovation is best achieved by collaboration of different agencies.

32. The aims and syllabus of the transition year are given in *Rules and Programme for Secondary Schools*. See also Egan, O., and O'Reilly, J. *The Transition Year Project*. Education Research Centre, St Patrick's College, Drumcondra, 1977. *Oideas*, No 20, 1977, contains a very useful summary of this report by the authors. *Compass*, Vol 5, No 2, 1976, contains a series of case studies on the transition year as does *The Extra Year: Enrichment in the School Curriculum* which was published by the Irish Association for Curriculum Development in 1983.

33. The Psychological Service, Department of Education *A Handbook on the PACE Programme*, 1980. See also an article on the programme by J Walsh and P O'Dwyer in the *Journal of the Institute of Guidance Counsellors*, Vol 5, Autumn, 1981.

34. See J. McKernan, "Organising for Curriculum Development" in *Compass*, Vol 10, No 2, 1981. Materials for years 1, 2 and 3 are now available privately from Tipperary (NR) VEC.

35. See O'Brien H. "Social and Health Education — The Development of a Programme for Junior Cycle Students". in *Compass*, Vol. 13, No. 1, (1984).

36. E. Donoghue, "Health Education in Schools", *Compass*, Vol 10, No 2, 1981.

37. See various issues of *School News*, published by the Health Education Bureau and the Volume 6, Spring, 1982, of the *Journal of the Institute of Guidance Counsellors*.

38. *The Social and Health Education Programme: A Handbook for Teachers and Other Educators*, Ógra Corcai, 1982.

39. J. Sheils, "The ITE Modern Languages Project: An Experiment in a Communicative Approach to Second Language Earnign" and J.L.M. Trim, "Modern Languages in the Council of Europe 1971/1981" in *Compass*, Vol. 11, No. 2, 1982. The first year materials and tapes have been published under the title *Salut* by the Education Company, Dublin.

40. See McLoone M., "Film and Media Studies" in *Compass*, Vol. 11, No. 1, (1982) and Annual Reports of the Curriculum Development Unit.

41. See Barry M. and Pollock H.M., "Industrial Relations and the Post-Primary School Student" in *Compass*, Vol. 11, No. 1, (1982).

42. See G. O'Flynn, "A Development Education Project" in *Compass*, Vol 10, No 2, 1981. The materials for the project will be published by O'Brien Educational in 1984.

43. This Network is coordinated by the CDVEC Curriculum Development Unit for the European Community. *Milieu* is the Newsletter of the Network and is published twice each year. Further information about the Network can be obtained from 28 Westland Row, Dublin 2.

44. Curriculum Development Associates Inc., *Man: A Course of Study*, 1971. This is one of the most influential curriculum projects at an international level because "it is an example of curriculum thinking made practice" (J Rudduck). A short description of the use of MACOS in Ireland by J A Crooks can be found in the *Proceedings of the Association for the Study of the Curriculum* (Norwich, 1975).

45. See Arts Council, *The Place of the Arts in Irish Education* (1979).

46. Irish Association for Curriculum Development, *The Extra Year: Enrichment in the School Curriculum* (1983).

47. County Tipperary (NR) VEC. *Post-Primary Education, 1985-2000, A Policy Document* (1979). County Monaghan V.E.C. Curriculum Report (1983).

48. Madaus, P. & MacNamara, J. *Public Examinations*. Education Research Centre: St. Patrick's College, Drumcondra, 1970.

49. *Final Report of the Committee on the Form and Function of the Intermediate Certificate Examination* (The Ice Report). Government Publications, 1975.

50. This project issued four reports which were published by the School of Education, Trinity College, Dublin. Heywood, J., *Assessment in History,* Report No. 1., 1974. Heywood, J., *Assessment in Mathematics,* Report No. 2, 1976. Heywood, J., McGuinness S., and Murphy, D., *The Public Examinations Evaluation Project: Progress Report* 1977. Heywood, J., McGuinness, S., Murphy, D., *The Public Examinations Evaluation Project Final Report.* 1980.

Chapter Two

1. Refer to Nie, N. Jenkins, Hull, C.H., J.G. Steinbrenner, K. and Bent, D.H. *Statistical Package for the Social Sciences,* 2nd Edition, New York: Mc Graw-Hill, 1975.
2. See Clarke, M.T. *Men, Women and Post-Primary Principalship in Northern Ireland.* Belfast: The Equal Opportunities Commission for Northern Ireland, 1978.

Chapter Three

1. For further discussion of educational reforms to achieve greater equality of educational opportunity see Chapter 1 of Mulcahy, D., *Curriculum and Policy in Irish Post Primary Education op. cit.,* and Randles, E. *Post-Primary Education in Ireland, 1957-70 op. cit.*
2. See for example, Whitehead, Alfred North, *The Aims of Education And Other Essays.* London: Ernest Benn, Ltd 1932, p. 21.

Chapter Four

1. For a detailed account of factors influencing curriculum innovations in American society, see Berman, P and McLoughlin, N A *Federal Programs Supporting Educational Change,* Los Angeles: Rand Corporation, 1975, Volumes 1 - IV.
2. An interesting discussion of curriculum constraints is contained in MacDonald, B., and Rudduck, J. "Curriculum research and development projects: barriers to success". *British Journal of Educational Psychology,* 44, 2, 148-154.
3. See "School-based curriculum development" by Malcolm Skilbeck. Open University Educational Studies — A second level course. Curriculum Design and Development, Unit 26 School Based Curriculum Development. Milton Keynes: O U Press, pp 90-103, 1976.
   See also Fullan, M. and Pomfret, A., "Research on Curriculum and Instruction Implementation", *Review of Educational Research,* 1977, Volume 47, 335-397.
4. There is also some research which has begun to explore the dynamics within institutions which inhibit planned change, for example, Gross, N. Gacquinta, J.B. and Bernstein, M., *Implementing Organisational Innovations.* New York: Harper, 1971.
5. See McKernan, J. "Constraints on the handling of controversial issues in Northern Ireland Post-Primary schools" *British Educational Research Journal,* Volume 18, No 1, 1982, pp 57-71.
6. Steadman, S et al. *The Schools Council, Its Takeup in Schools and General Impact,* Final Report: London Schools Council: 1981.

Chapter Five

1. Several studies have concerned themselves with the effects of transfer on pupils and the dynamics of the transfer procedure. See Nisbet, J and Entwistle, N J *The Transition to Secondary Education.* Publication No 59, 1969, Scottish Council for Educational Research, London: U of London Press, Also, Nisbet, J and Entwistle, N J *The Age of Transfer,* 1966. Also, Youngman, M B and Lunzer, E *Adjustment to Secondary Schooling.* School of Education, Nottingham University 1977.

2. See two interesting postgraduate theses: O'Flaherty, J "Transition to post-primary education". Master of Education thesis, Education Department, University College, Galway, 1977. Also Doyle, A "Transition from primary to post-primary education: a case study of the main problems with particular reference to geography. M.Ed. Thesis, Education Department, U.C.D., 1982.

3. See *The Report of the Committee on Pupil Transfer.* Dublin: The Stationery Office, 1982.

4. Doyle, A. *op. cit.*

5. See Nisbet, J and Entwistle, W.J. (1966) and (1969) *op. cit.* for a discussion of these studies conducted on a sample of Aberdeen pupils.

6. Two studies which provide empirical data related to the transfer of pupils in Northern Ireland are: Spelman, B J *Pupil Adaptation to Secondary School,* No 18 Northern Ireland Council for Educational Research, 1979 and McKernan, J *Transfer at 14,* Belfast: NICER, 1981.

7. Department of Education. *The Ages of Learning* Dublin, The Stationery Office, 1984.

8. See for example, Kelly, A.V. 'Mixed Ability Grouping: Theory with Practice.' *Compass,* Volume 9, No 1, 1980.

9. See Barker Lunn, Joan C., *Streaming in the Primary School.* Slough: National Foundation for Educational Research, 1970, for a study of English pupils.
    In Sweden, research by Husen, T and Svenssen, Nile, E. "Pedagogic milieu and development of intellectual skills *School Review,* Vol. 68, 36-51, 1960.
    In the USA, research by Goldberg, M and Passow, H *The Effects of Ability Grouping: A Comparative study of broad, medium and narrow range closes in the elementary school.* New York: Teachers College, Columbia University, 1965.

10. See Daniels, J.C., "The Effects of streaming in two primary schools," *British Journal of Educational Psychology,* Vol. 31, 69-78, 1961, and Borg, W.R., "Ability grouping in the public schools", *Journal of Experimental Education,* 34, 2, 1-97, 1965.

11. Elder, G.H. "Life opportunity and personality: some consequences of stratified secondary education in Great Britain", *Sociology of Education,* 1965, 38, 173-202.

12. Barker Lunn, J.C., *Streaming In the Primary School, op. cit.*

13. The following definitions are based on the *International Dictionary of Education.* London: Kogan Page, by G Terry, Page, J B Thomas, and A Marshall.
    Streaming is the practice of dividing all the children of the same particular chronological age into separate classes on the basis of general ability.
    Mixed Ability Grouping is the practice in which the full range of ability is represented with the exception of pupils requiring special education. Mixed ability may refer to a class of pupils, a year group, or the entire school.
    Banding is the broad form of grouping pupils in school by ability. Pupils in a year may be split equally into two or more bands of higher or lower ability; then, from within each of the two (or more) bands, two or more classes may be formed each containing pupils of the highest and lowest ability within that band. This represents a compromise between streaming and mixed ability grouping.
    Setting is the division of pupils of a particular age group into sets according to ability in particular subjects. Thus a pupil may be in the top set for Maths and in the third set for French.

14. McKernan, J *Transfer at 14, op. cit.,* pp 73-82.

15. See Department of Education, *Rules and Programmes for Secondary Schools,* Dublin: The Stationery Office, 1983.

16. A national survey of reading standards in post-primary schools (1971-1972) was carried out by Swan, D. *Reading Standards In Irish Schools.* Dublin: The Educational Company, 1978.

APPENDIX

Principals' Questionnaire for Post-Primary Schools in Ireland

Curriculum Development in Schools

Irish Association for Curriculum Development
1, Bellevue Road, Glenageary, Co. Dublin.

NATIONAL SURVEY OF CURRICULUM DEVELOPMENT IN IRISH POST-PRIMARY SCHOOLS

We would be most grateful for your help in completing the following questionnaire to help in a survey of curriculum change and development in Irish post-primary schools in recent years, including present practice and future directions. By the term 'curriculum' we mean the totality of learning experiences to which the pupil is exposed at school or in association with the school. These learning experiences are taken to mean not only the range of subjects with their individual syllabi, including knowledge, skills and attitudes, but also informal educational experiences organized by the school. By 'curriculum development' we mean deliberate attempts to improve the curriculum by adopting, adapting, rejecting or generating curriculum change in the school.

The survey is being carried out by the Irish Association for Curriculum Development and has the support of the Department of Education. We realize the many demands that are made upon Principals' time, yet as you will understand, research plays a vital role in curriculum planning and it is essential to understand how principals of post-primary schools feel about curriculum development.

The questionnaire is in five parts:

PART 1 requests information on curriculum development in recent years. This section will focus on curriculum innovations introduced by the Government Department of Education; locally-based schemes, and projects developed with support structures outside of the school.

PART 2 will examine the desired curriculum changes that you would like to see implemented in the curriculum of the future.

PART 3 requests information relating to the barriers, or constraints that may be placed upon curriculum development in your school.

PART 4 will focus upon present organizational arrangements regarding such issues as: pupil transfer from primary to post-primary school; modes of grouping pupils for instruction, and pupil participation in public examinations.

PART 5 seeks certain biographical and background information relating to your school. These details are necessary for the analysis of data and will be treated with absolute confidentiality. We wish to emphasise that the questionnaire is anonymous. No individual or school will be identified or identifiable in any reports of our work. We are interested in the general patterns that emerge from the analysis of data provided by principals, and not in the replies of any particular schools. At no time will any attempt be made to breach this principle of anonymity. Your cooperation is vital to the success of the project.

Please complete the questionnaire in private, which should then be sealed in the envelope provided and returned to:

The Irish Association for Curriculum Development,
1, Bellevue Road,
Glenageary,
Dun Laoghaire,
Co. Dublin.

SECTION 1: CURRICULUM DEVELOPMENT IN RECENT YEARS

This section deals with the new programmes that have been started in your school in recent years.

NEW COURSES AT NATIONAL LEVEL

Since 1970 several new courses have been introduced by the Department of Education and are available to all schools or to all schools of a particular type.

Col. 5

1. Does your school offer a Pre-Employment Course?   YES   2
   (Please circle one number)   NO   1

6

2. Has your school offered this course in the past?   YES   2
   (Please circle one number)   NO   1

7-10

3. In what year was the Pre-Employment Course first introduced in your school? *(Please enter year)* ———

11

4. If your school currently does not offer a Pre-Employment Course, would your school like to offer a Pre-Employment Course?   YES   2
   NO   1

5. The following subjects have been introduced at Leaving Certificate level since 1969-70. Does your school currently teach these subjects, and if so, in what year were the subjects first introduced?
(Please tick / the appropriate box)

	YES	NO	YEAR	
Technical Drawing				12-13
Economic History				14-15
Engineering Workshop Theory				16-17
Building Construction				18-19
Accountancy				20-21
Business Organization				22-23
Home Economics (Scientific/Social)				24-25
Home Economics (General)				26-27
Agricultural Economics				28-29
Economics				30-31
Mechanics				32-33

6. The Department of Education have introduced certain courses, or modules of courses e.g. Classical Studies, Computer Module in Maths, etc. Please name which courses of this type are taught in your school.

———————————————————————

———————————————————————

———————————————————————

34-35

SCHOOL-BASED CURRICULUM DEVELOPMENT SCHEMES

A school-based curriculum development project, or experimental teaching scheme, is one originating in your own school, or in a group of schools nearby. It might be concerned with the teaching of a particular subject, or area, such as Local History, or, be a new subject added to the curriculum of one or more schools. A school-based curriculum development might also involve the trial of experimental teaching strategies viz. role-playing, or involve a restructuring of the pupils' working day. The scheme could require some new type of classroom organization such as team-teaching or mixed-ability grouping. Such a development could also take the form of some new mode of assessment of pupils' work. In terms of subjects, it might take the form of a course such as Pastoral Care, or Media Studies.

7. Since 1970, have you, or members of your staff, taken part in any school-based curriculum development project, or experimental teaching scheme, as defined above, which was not listed in the previous section?
   (Please circle one number)   YES   2

                                         NO   1

   36

8. If your answer to item 7 was yes, please complete the next five items. Please name the scheme(s) and add a brief description if its (their) nature is not clear from the title.

   _____

   37-38

   _____

   _____

9. Where did the scheme(s) originate?

   39

10. Is it supported by any outside agency e.g. Teacher Centre, Teacher-Training Institution, etc.)?
    YES   YES   2

                                         NO   1

    Please indicate type of support agency. _____

    40

    41

    _____

11. Are you, or members of your staff, using the scheme(s) this year? YES   2
    (Please circle one number)
                                                     NO   1

    42

12. Have any other schools been involved in the project or scheme(s)? YES   3

                                         DONT KNOW   2

                                         NO   1

    43

13. Does your school have a programme for children with special needs? *(Please circle one number)*   YES   2

                                         NO   1

14. If your school has a programme for children with special needs, viz. handicapped pupils, or pupils of exceptional ability, please describe the programme(s).

    _____

    _____

    _____

    _____

**FORMAL CURRICULUM DEVELOPMENT PROJECTS
(supported by official agencies)**

Off. Use

15. Please record your familiarity with any of the curriculum projects listed below by circling the appropriate number. In responding, use the following keys:

I am unfamiliar with the project *(circle number 1)*
I have heard of the project *(circle number 2)*
Have used materials or project ideas *(circle number 3)*
Have been a pilot school for the project *(circle number 4)*
Am currently involved with the project *(circle number 5)*

City of Dublin Humanities Project (C.D.U.)*	1	2	3	4	5	47
Early School Leavers Project (C.D.U.)	1	2	3	4	5	48
Education for Development (North Mayo Curriculum Project)	1	2	3	4	5	49
Health Education (Health Education Bureau)	1	2	3	4	5	50
Institiuid Teangeolaiochta Eireann (Modern Languages) ...	1	2	3	4	5	51
Irish Studies (Department of Education)	1	2	3	4	5	52
ISCIP Integrated Science Curr. Innovation Project (CDU)	1	2	3	4	5	53
Nua Chursa Gaeilge (Department of Education)	1	2	3	4	5	54
Outdoor Education Project (C.D.U.)	1	2	3	4	5	55
SESP Social and Environmental Studies Project (Shannon)	1	2	3	4	5	56
SPIRAL (Shannon Project of Interventions for Relevant Adolescent Learnings)	1	2	3	4	5	57
Transition Year Project (Department of Education) ...	1	2	3	4	5	58
Others (please identify, including projects from overseas)	1	2	3	4	5	59

*Curriculum Development Unit, VEC/TCD

**SECTION 2:
DESIRED CURRICULUM CHANGES / INNOVATIONS
IN THE FUTURE**

Col.

In this section we are interested in finding out what particular curriculum changes you would like to see in the foreseeable future. Such changes might take the form of: revision of syllabi; development of new teaching materials, subjects, teaching styles, and modes of pupil assessment or course evaluation. On the other hand such changes might involve the use of new equipment and apparatus, etc., that you would welcome in your school.

16. Are there any subjects or topics not presently taught in your school that you would like to see included in the formal curriculum? *(Please circle one number)*

YES   2   60

NO   1

17. If your answer to item 16 was yes, what are these subjects?   61-62

_____

_____

			Off. Use
18. Are there any subjects taught in your school that you feel have little or no value? *(Please circle one number)*			
	YES	2	63
	NO	1	

19. If your answer to item 18 was yes, please name these subjects.   64-65

_____

_____

20. Would you like to see greater teacher involvement in the assessment of their own pupils in connection with public examinations? *(Please circle one number)*			66
	YES	2	
	NO	1	

21. If your answer to item 20 was Yes, what form would this teacher involvement take? (e.g. assessment of coursework, practical work, etc.)   67

_____

_____

_____

Col.

22. To what extent do you agree that the curriculum of your own school should be the subject of continuous review and development? *(Please circle one number)*

I strongly agree	5	
I agree to some extent	4	68
I am uncertain	3	
I disagree to some extent	2	
I strongly disagree	1	69-71

Card 2
Col. 1-4

23. With regard to curriculum change, do you feel that post-primary education in Ireland needs: *(Please circle one number)*

Major Changes	5	
Some Changes	4	
Uncertain of Changes	3	5
Hardly any Changes	2	
No Changes	1	

24. Far more changes ought to have been made in the post-primary curriculum in recent years. *(Please circle one number)*

I Strongly Agree	5	
I agree to some extent	4	
I am uncertain	3	6
I disagree to some extent	2	
I strongly disagree	1	

Sources of Teacher Support
We are interested in finding out how important/unimportant the following factors are
in supporting teachers involved in curriculum development. Please consider each type
of teacher support by looking at the scale under the item and by circling the number
that comes closest to your own feeling about the importance of the factor in helping
teachers. "I" means that you think the factor is *very unimportant,* "7" means that you
think the factor *very important* in supporting teachers. Please circle one number for
each item in order of importance.

Off. Use

Col.

| 25. | SUPPORT FROM THE PRINCIPAL | | | | | | | 7 |

| | | Very | Quite | Slightly | Equally | Slightly | Quite | Very | |
| Unimportant | 1 | 2 | 3 | 4 | 5 | 6 | 7 | Important |

26. SHORT INSERVICE COURSES — 8

| | Very | Quite | Slightly | Equally | Slightly | Quite | Very | |
| Unimportant | 1 | 2 | 3 | 4 | 5 | 6 | 7 | Important |

27. TEACHER RELEASE TO STUDY AT THIRD LEVEL INSTITUTION — 9

| | Very | Quite | Slightly | Equally | Slightly | Quite | Very | |
| Unimportant | 1 | 2 | 3 | 4 | 5 | 6 | 7 | Important |

28. STAFF/DEPARTMENT MEETINGS ON CURRICULUM MATTERS
AT SCHOOL — 10

| | Very | Quite | Slightly | Equally | Slightly | Quite | Very | |
| Unimportant | 1 | 2 | 3 | 4 | 5 | 6 | 7 | Important |

29. REGULAR MEETINGS WITH TEACHERS FROM OTHER SCHOOLS — 11

| | Very | Quite | Slightly | Equally | Slightly | Quite | Very | |
| Unimportant | 1 | 2 | 3 | 4 | 5 | 6 | 7 | Important |

30. CURRICULUM MATERIALS / PACKAGES FROM EXTERNAL SOURCES — 12

| | Very | Quite | Slightly | Equally | Slightly | Quite | Very |
| Unimportant | 1 | 2 | 3 | 4 | 5 | 6 | 7 |

31. REGULAR RELEASE FROM TEACHING TO PLAN THE CURRICULUM
(ONE OR TWO PERIODS PER WEEK: PLANNING MEETINGS) — 13

| | Very | Quite | Slightly | Equally | Slightly | Quite | Very | |
| Unimportant | 1 | 2 | 3 | 4 | 5 | 6 | 7 | Important |

32. EDUCATIONAL JOURNALS / MAGAZINES AND OTHER PRINTED MATTER — 14

| | Very | Quite | Slightly | Equally | Slightly | Quite | Very | |
| Unimportant | 1 | 2 | 3 | 4 | 5 | 6 | 7 | Important |

33. ADVICE OF INSPECTORATE — 15

| | Very | Quite | Slightly | Equally | Slightly | Quite | Very | |
| Unimportant | 1 | 2 | 3 | 4 | 5 | 6 | 7 | Important |

34. Please list in the space provided below any other factors that you consider to be
supporting of teacher involvement in curriculum development which have not been
included in the above section.

16-17

_____

_____

_____

35. With regard to inservice education, what things should be done to benefit teachers in
your school?

Col.

18-19

_____

_____

_____   _____

Off. **Use**

36. Please feel free to comment on the types of curriculum changes that you would like to see in the post-primary curriculum of the future.

20-21

_____

_____

_____

SECTION 3: CONSTRAINTS ON CURRICULUM DEVELOPMENT

In this section we are interested in finding out how important/unimportant the list of constraints, or barriers, identified below, are on curriculum development in your school. Study each constraint carefully and then circle the number that comes closest to your own personal opinion about the importance of the constraints in your school. "1" means the constraint is _very unimportant_, "7" indicates that it is _very important_ as an impediment to curriculum development. Circle one number for each item in order of importance.

37.   THE EXAMINATION SYSTEM   22
              Very   Quite Slightly Equally Slightly Quite Very
Unimportant   1   2   3   4   5   6   7   Important

38.   FINANCIAL REASONS / COSTS   23
              Very   Quite Slightly Equally Slightly Quite Very
Unimportant   1   2   3   4   5   6   7   Important

39.   LACK OF INSERVICE TRAINING   24
              Very   Quite Slightly Equally Slightly Quite Very
Unimportant   1   2   3   4   5   6   7   Important

40.   LACK OF COMMITMENT OF TEACHERS   25
              TO CURRICULUM DEVELOPMENT
              Very   Quite Slightly Equally Slightly Quite Very
Unimportant   1   2   3   4   5   6   7   Important

41.   LACK OF TIME TO IMPLEMENT INNOVATIONS PROPERLY   26
              Very   Quite Slightly Equally Slightly Quite Very
Unimportant   1   2   3   4   5   6   7   Important

42.   ORGANIZATIONAL ARRANGEMENTS / STRUCTURE OF SCHOOL   Col.
              Very   Quite Slightly Equally Slightly Quite Very
Unimportant   1   2   3   4   5   6   7   Important   27

43.   LACK OF PARENTAL SUPPORT
              Very   Quite Slightly Equally Slightly Quite Very   28
Unimportant   1   2   3   4   5   6   7   Important

44.   LACK OF RESOURCES/FACILITIES/MATERIALS
              Very   Quite Slightly Equally Slightly Quite Very   29
Unimportant   1   2   3   4   5   6   7   Important

45.   RULES AND PROGRAMMES FOR SCHOOLS
              Very   Quite Slightly Equally Slightly Quite Very   30
Unimportant   1   2   3   4   5   6   7   Important

									Off. Use

46.   SCHOOL MANAGEMENT

	Very	Quite	Slightly	Equally	Slightly	Quite	Very		31
Unimportant	1	2	3	4	5	6	7	Important	

47.   TEACHERS' LACK OF KNOWLEDGE OR SKILLS

	Very	Quite	Slightly	Equally	Slightly	Quite	Very		32
Unimportant	1	2	3	4	5	6	7	Important	

48.   TEACHER-PUPIL RATIO

	Very	Quite	Slightly	Equally	Slightly	Quite	Very		33
Unimportant	1	2	3	4	5	6	7	Important	

49. Please specify any other constraint on curriculum development not mentioned above.

_____   34-35

_____

50. As you see it, what are the three most important constraints on curriculum development in your school? (Please rank in order of importance)

(1) _____   36

(2) _____   37

(3) _____   38

SECTION 4: ORGANIZATIONAL ARRANGEMENTS

Col.

In this section we wish to inquire into certain curricular arrangements, viz. pupil transfer, modes of grouping pupils for instruction, and pupil participation in public examinations.

51. Do you have arrangements with primary schools concerning pupil transfer?
(Please circle one number)

YES	2	39
NO	1	

52. If Yes, please describe these arrangements._____   40-41

_____

53. How satisfied are you with present arrangements for pupil transfer from primary to post-primary schooling? *(please circle one number)*

Extremely satisfied	5
Fairly satisfied	4
I am uncertain	3
Fairly dissatisfied	2
Very dissatisfied	1

42

54. Why? _____   43

_____

_____

55. Is the present age of transfer from primary to post-primary school right for the
majority of pupils? *(Circle one number)*

YES	3
UNCERTAIN	2
NO	1

56. If No, what age do you believe is best for pupil transfer? Please indicate age in years.

_____years of age is best.

57. Is there a need for closer alignment between the curricula of primary and post-
primary schools? *(Please circle one number)*

YES	3
UNCERTAIN	2
NO	1

58. If Yes, how could closer alignment be achieved?

_____

_____

59. How are most pupils grouped in your school?

    (a)   pupils are grouped by ability
         (streaming)   1

    (b)   pupils of different abilities are
         taught together
         (mixed-ability)   2

    (c)   other (please specify)   3

_____

60. If pupils are streamed, by ability, is this done at all grade levels?

YES	2
NO	1

If No, please describe below:

_____

_____

61. If pupils are streamed, what criteria are used to determine pupil allocation to stream?

_____

_____

62. If your pupils are grouped by ability (streamed), why is this practised in your school?

_____

_____

63. What percentage of the pupils who enter your school sit for the **Group Certificate**
AFTER: *(circle number)*

TWO YEARS		THREE YEARS	
NONE	1	NONE	1
1-25%	2	1-25%	2
26-50%	3	26-50%	3
51-75%	4	51-75%	4
76-99%	5	76-99%	5
ALL	6	ALL	6

64. What percentage of the pupils who enter your school sit for the **Intermediate
Certificate** AFTER: *(circle number)*

THREE YEARS		FOUR YEARS	
NONE	1	NONE	1
1-25%	2	1-25%	2
26-50%	3	26-50%	3
51-75%	4	51-75%	4
76-99%	5	76-99%	5
ALL	6	ALL	6

65. What percentage of pupils who enter the **senior cycle** sit for the **Leaving Certificate**
AFTER: *(circle number)*

TWO YEARS		THREE YEARS	
NONE	1	NONE	1
1-25%	2	1-25%	2
26-50%	3	26-50%	3
51-75%	4	51-75%	4
76-99%	5	76-99%	5
ALL	6	ALL	6

66. What percentage of the pupils never sit a public examination?   %
(Please enter approximate percentage)

67. What percentage of pupils leave school after completion of the **junior cycle?**   %
(Please enter percentage)

68. What other examinations are done in your school? *(Please specify)*

_____

_____

69. Does your school have: *(Please tick box)*

	YES	NO	IF YES, HOW MANY?
Whole Time Guidance Teacher			
Part-Time Guidance Teacher			

If No, do you need a Guidance Teacher?
(Please circle)   YES   2

                    NO   1

70. Does your school have:

	YES	NO	IF YES, HOW MANY?
Whole Time Remedial Teacher			
Part-Time Remedial Teacher			

70-71

If No, do you need a Remeidal Teacher?
(Please circle one number)   YES   2   72

NO   1

71. How satisfied are you with present provision for: Col.
(Please circle appropriate numbers)

	Guidance	Remedial Ed.	Physical Ed.
Extremely satisfied	5	5	5
Satisfied	4	4	4
Uncertain	3	3	3
Fairly Dissatisfied	2	2	2
Extremely dissatisfied	1	1	1

73-75

Card 3
Col. 1-4

SECTION 5: BACKGROUND AND DEMOGRAPHIC INFORMATION

For each of the following queries, *please circle the appropriate number,* except where otherwise indicated.

72. TYPE OF SCHOOL

	Boys	Girls	Co-ed
Secondary	1	2	3
Comprehensive	1	2	3
Community	1	2	3
Vocational	1	2	3

5

73. SIZE OF SCHOOL *(Circle number please)*

0 – 100	...	1
101 – 250	...	2
251 – 400	...	3
401 – 600	...	4
601 – 800	...	5
801 – 1000	...	6
1001 – 1250	...	7
OVER 1250	...	8

6

74. GEOGRAPHIC LOCATION OF THE SCHOOL

Is the school located in: An Urban Area (City/Town) 2   7
A Rural Area (Under 5,000) 1

75. NUMBER OF TEACHERS: *(Please enter number)*

Full-Time _____   8-9

Part-Time _____   10-11

76. ARE YOU: *(Please circle one number)*

MALE	2
FEMALE	1

Off. Use

12

77. SCHOOL MANAGEMENT: *(Please circle number)*

RELIGIOUS MANAGEMENT

Nuns	3
Priests	2
Brothers	1

13

LAY MANAGEMENT

Vocational Education Committee	4
Management Board	3
Governors	2
Other (specify)	1

14

78. AGE:

Are you:

25-30 years of age	1
31-40 years of age	2
41-50 years of age	3
51-60 years of age	4
Over 60 years of age	5

15

79. COMMENTS

In the space below please feel free to comment on any aspect of curriculum development, or any other issue which you feel has not been covered adequately by this questionnaire.

16-20

_____

_____

_____

_____

THANK YOU FOR YOUR HELP

LIST OF TABLES

INDEX